The Odd Couple
I and II

The Original Screenplays

Neil Simon

A Touchstone Book
Published by Simon & Schuster
New York   London   Sydney   Singapore

TOUCHSTONE
Rockefeller Center
1230 Avenue of the Americas
New York, NY 10020

TOUCHSTONE and colophon are registered trademarks
of Simon & Schuster Inc.

Designed by Gabriel Levine

Manufactured in the United States of America

10 9 8 7 6 5 4 3 2 1

Library of Congress Cataloging-in-Publication Data

Simon, Neil.
[Odd couple (Screenplay)]
The odd couple I and II: the original screen plays / Neil Simon.
p. cm.
"A Touchstone book."
Contents: Introduction—The odd couple—The odd couple II: travelin' light.
I. Title: Odd couple 1 and 2. II. Title: Odd couple one and two. III. Simon, Neil. Odd
couple II. IV. Title.

PN1997.O184   2000
791.43'75—dc21

99-052814

ISBN 0-684-85925-4

To Danny Simon and Roy Gerber

Contents

A Couple of Odd Couples

Anyone who has ever read anything about my career probably knows the oft-told story of how *The Odd Couple* was born. The birth was the result of the union of my brother Danny and his friend Roy Gerber, an agent, who, in the early sixties, were each divorced. They decided to move in together to save expenses, helping to defray the costs of alimony, which they were both paying. What inevitably happened to these new roommates is that the fights and squabbles they had recently left behind, after their marital breakups, suddenly resurfaced in their own new relationship in the apartment they now shared. The odd thing about this odd couple was that Roy and Danny were having the same problems with each other as they did with their wives. Perhaps worse. The point being that if you have annoying traits, habits and idiosyncrasies, you bring them with you no matter where you go. Felix (my brother Danny) was the stereotypical "housewife," who puffs up cushions immediately after someone gets up from a chair or tells you to eat your slice of pizza over the dish to avoid leaving crumbs on the floor. Oscar (Roy Gerber) was the complete opposite. He would rather leave crumbs on the floor well past the following Christmas than to get out a vacuum cleaner, which was probably broken from lack of use. Hence an idea was born. Then it was written, rehearsed, put on a Broadway stage, transferred to the screen by Paramount Pictures, then made into a television series that has been roaming around the world, day and night, for the past thirty years and will probably continue to do so for at least another thirty years. There is hardly a single day that *The Odd Couple* isn't playing somewhere in the world. It was a natural from the day it was born.

Eventually it spawned a female counterpart, not so ironically called *The Female Odd Couple*. It was virtually the same play, the same situations, only I rewrote the dialogue completely to be sure this was a play about women, who no doubt suffered the same traits, habits and idiosyncrasies as men. And were no more patient in dealing with it.

As the years went on and the play showed no sign of slowing down, I began to wonder, why this longevity? Why is it still being played in theaters all over the world, translated into every language possible and often repeated in those same theaters like clockwork every few years? Each new generation was brought to the play by their parents or possibly saw the original film on television. It suddenly occurred to me. It's not so much that audiences wanted to *see* it. The answer was that so many people wanted to *play* it. Every actor or would-be actor, every high school student, college student, every salesman or dentist, every hairstylist or schoolteacher wanted to play Oscar or Felix, or Olive and Florence. Schools do it constantly, breeding as many Oscars and Felixes as fast as the giant pods produced human counterparts in *The Invasion of the Body Snatchers*. Samuel French, the company that leases the play on my behalf, sends me its royalty statements periodically. In almost every statement *The Odd Couple* and now *The Female Odd Couple* outdistances all my other plays by a wide margin. Amateur groups are probably the largest source of requests to do either of the two plays. For years now, people stop me on the street or in a restaurant and say in passing, "Hi, Mr. Simon, I was Oscar in high school," or a middle-aged woman extolls her personal joys in having performed Olive in *The Female Odd Couple*.

The first *Odd Couple* film still shows its stage origins. The play, obviously, was written for the stage and I felt there was no need to intrude too many outdoor locations. The two men, in a sense, were trapped together in a five-room apartment and that was the battlefield for their daily encounters. From breakfast to dinner, from morning till night, they couldn't pass each other anywhere in the apartment without incident. It was the arena for their daily, almost nonstop irritations. Felix complained of Oscar's cigar, which fell out of the ashtray, probably on purpose. Oscar bemoaned Felix's clearing of his sinuses, usually at two in the morning, making a sound that was annoyingly similar to a moose call in Canada.

Its universality is obvious. Who among us, sometime in his life, hasn't shared living quarters with another human being? It didn't matter whether they liked each other or not. Eventually their silent anger became audible, complaining how one whistled in the kitchen, and usually the same awful tune, while the other one claimed control of the TV clicker and blipped through a hundred stations in six seconds constantly through the night. Who hasn't experienced sheer hatred for the sounds his roommate made while he was eating? The play represented everyone in the world, including, I imagine, astronauts in space for weeks at a time.

The title was the first thing I thought of but was almost vetoed by my producer for fear people would think this was a gay play. In 1964, it would be hard to find a gay play and gays weren't actually called gays as yet. I fought for my title primarily because it was already part of our language. A short husband married to a taller wife would immediately be dubbed an odd couple. For a play, the name was easy to remember. What I never anticipated was that, in due time, it became a phrase no longer used for its original meaning. Once the play reached the stage and the film opened in movie houses (both enormous hits), when someone said "the odd couple" for its original intent, it was taken as a reference to the theatrical *Odd Couple.* It suddenly was appearing in magazines and newspapers. We would see the president of the United States shaking hands with a smiling ruler of Russian, and the caption underneath the photo told us this was "The Odd Couple." For thirty-five years now I have been receiving free publicity, all over the world, for a phrase I borrowed from the English language. To a lesser degree, a photo of two elderly men smiling at the beach was sometimes captioned, "The Sunshine Boys." I've seen small motels around the country called "Plaza Suites." I've never claimed title or royalties for that. I just liked that they were putting the name of my play and film into the audience's minds. A picture in the sports pages of a New York Yankee watching a ball going out of sight over the left field fence has the caption underneath saying, "Lost in Yonkers." A warning to other writers: If you plan to use the colloquial English language as a title, make sure your play or movie is a very good and popular work. Just titles don't cut it.

If this were 1967 instead of 1999, *The Odd Couple* would have made a perfect sequel on the heels of the first one. Only sequels weren't being made back then. Think of all the *Batman* pictures that would not have been made, of the Indiana Jones follow-ups we would have missed or the *Star*

Trek sequels that are being rolled out as I write this. I'll leave the judgment issue of those films to the reader. I'm not a critic. I wish *The Odd Couple II was* made back then because Walter and Jack would have been younger men and the picture would have had the same energy as the first one. If you missed *The Odd Couple II* at your local Cineplex, see how it reads instead of how it was on the screen. But to make it work in your heads, you must visualize Walter as Oscar and Jack as Felix.

When we made the sequel, we were facing another problem. Prior to filming, Walter and Jack had made *Grumpy Old Men,* which was quite funny, then *Grumpier Old Men,* which was also quite good, followed by *Out to Sea.* In a sense they're all spinoffs of *The Odd Couple* but I take no umbrage. Mostly because no one sent me any. But I think being last on line after three previous movies with Walter and Jack playing ostensibly the same kind of characters, and then following up with *The Odd Couple II,* was a bridge too far. There was still one more problem. Anyone from the ages of ten to forty grew up with Jack Klugman and Tony Randall being Oscar and Felix on TV, and damn brilliantly, I might add. So what, asked the younger generation, were Walter and Jack doing in *The Odd Couple?* I can understand their plight.

Today *The Odd Couple* proliferates on TV screens from the networks to cable, under different names and different combinations of people, all living in the same apartment, house or office, much younger but doing, to some degree, what Walter and Jack did thirty some years ago. I don't watch them because there's usually a basketball or baseball game on somewhere. I don't get royalties, but hey, how much did Shakespeare make out of *Shakespeare in Love?* Not a farthing, I guess, but it was good publicity for him.

The two *Odd Couple*s are not the only films I made with Walter and Jack. I guess I did about five each with one acting without the other. Everyone should be so lucky. I loved every minute of each film but I would have to honestly say that the success of *The Odd Couple* movie is probably the greatest thrill I've had in my career.

This introduction was written on a typewriter. There are some things a writer just hates giving up.

Neil Simon
April 1999
Los Angeles

The Odd Couple

EXT. THE MID-FORTIES BETWEEN 6TH AND 7TH AVENUES—IT IS HOT AND HUMID—NIGHT

It is a block filled with Chili restaurants, parking lots and third-rate hotels. Into view comes FELIX UNGAR, walking aimlessly along the street. He wears a tan linen suit, rumpled, his tie is askew and his top button on his shirt is open. His eyes are bleary and ringed with a lack of sleep. His hands are in his pockets and he walks without purpose and in no particular direction. He is oblivious to the world around him. Suddenly his eyes squint at the glare of an electric sign on top of the marquee of a small, cheap hotel. Felix stops and looks up to the top of the hotel. He turns and looks around the street . . . possibly a last look at a world that doesn't seem to need or want him. He enters the hotel.

INT. HOTEL—NIGHT

The seedy lobby is empty except for a desk clerk eating a pizza pie from a hot metal plate. Felix is clearly uncomfortable in this unpleasant atmosphere. He crosses to the desk.

FELIX
I'd . . . I'd like a room, please.

The desk clerk looks at him, puts the pizza plate on a shelf under the desk, wipes his hands on his pants and looks at Felix.

CLERK

Alone?

(Felix nods)

Luggage?

(Felix shakes his head 'no')

How long you want it for?

FELIX

... Not very long.

CLERK

Six dollars.

Felix takes a few bills out of his pocket and gives them to the clerk, who reaches back and gets a key and hands it to Felix. Felix signs register.

CLERK

Three oh seven.

FELIX

... Don't you have anything higher?

The clerk looks at Felix. He takes back the key and hands Felix another key.

CLERK

Nine fourteen?

Felix nods. Felix walks into the small self-service elevator. The door closes.

INT. ELEVATOR—NIGHT

Felix appears quite uneasy as he rides up to the ninth floor.

INT. NINTH FLOOR HALL

The elevator door opens and Felix gets out. He walks toward the direction of his room. In the foreground there is a cleaning woman wringing out several mops. She looks up at Felix.

CLEANING WOMAN
Good night.

FELIX
Good-bye.

He closes the door and the cleaning woman stops and looks back, extremely concerned.

INT. HOTEL ROOM—NIGHT

It is a small, depressing room with a single bed, a small bathroom and a window that faces out toward Times Square. Felix looks around the room. He sighs in despair. This is what he's come to. He crosses to the window and pulls up the shade. He crosses to desk and sits and takes out his wallet. He removes a picture and looks at it.

CLOSE-UP—FELIX

He puts picture back in wallet, places wallet on desk, removes his wristwatch, puts it on desk, takes off a wedding band and puts it on desk. He takes an envelope from desk and writes on it.

CLOSE SHOT OF ENVELOPE

Felix has written, "To my Wife and Beloved Children."

INT. HOTEL ROOM—FELIX—NIGHT

He places the items in the envelope, seals it and places it carefully tilted on top of the desk. He sighs and crosses to the window.

At the window, Felix adjusts his tie, smooths his hair with his hands and buttons his jacket. The window is closed. Felix puts his hands on the middle bar and pushes up, but the window is stuck. He tries harder but to no avail.

He then puts his hands on the bottom molding where the two handles are, sets his feet, and in one great effort, pulls up. The window still doesn't budge but Felix grimaces in excruciating pain as something must have snapped in his back. His hand goes to his back as he stamps around the room and finally falls onto the bed, twisted and wracked in pain. Things like this only happen to Felix Ungar. Even his final moment is a failure.

The titles begin.

EXT. SEVENTH AVENUE IN UPPER FORTIES—NIGHT

The streets are crowded with people. It's about ten o'clock.
Intersperse titles.

FELIX

is walking down the street, a little wearier looking than before. Occasionally he indicates his back is still giving him trouble. Especially when he bumps into people.

EXT. METROPOLE CAFE—NIGHT

The Metropole is a former jazz joint on Seventh Avenue that is now a discotheque for passersby. Four or five GO-GO-GIRLS entice the customers by dancing on top of the bar. If you have the price of a drink, you go in. If not, you join the throng of gawkers who assemble on the sidewalk peeking in.

FELIX

stands in the front of the crowd looking in. The people behind him shout to get out of the way. A Pinkerton policeman conducts traffic in front of bar, keeping the passersby moving. Felix steps forward to get out of way of crowd behind him and the Pinkerton man thinks Felix wants to go in so he ushers him quickly inside and goes back to his traffic. Before Felix realizes it, he's inside the bar.

INT. METROPOLE CAFE—NIGHT

The music, of course, is so loud, it's deafening. The bosomy girls are doing the thing they do on top of the bar. Felix lips his order to the bartender who pours him a drink in a shot glass. The girls dance directly over Felix.

GIRL DIRECTLY OVERHEAD

She dances with that noncommittal look of boredom.

FELIX

He has his drink in hand. He finds it difficult to look up at the girl because she is dancing so close to him, he is embarrassed. But his eyes finally make their way up to the girl.

GIRL DANCING ON BAR

She is dancing, still noncommittally. Then she looks down at Felix and purses her lips quickly at him. It's not a kiss. It's something else.

FELIX

His reaction is disgust. He throws his head back quickly to drink it all, western style, and in so doing, snaps his neck in pain and the drink mostly goes all over his front. He wipes himself off sheepishly and retreats from the cafe, his neck twisted in pain at a slightly odd angle.

EXT. HUDSON RIVER NEAR 79TH STREET BOAT BASIN—NIGHT

Felix stops at the rail and looks down into the water.

MED. SHOT—WATER

It is dark, murky and garbage floats on the top. It sloshes against the bank.

CLOSE-UP—FELIX

He reaches for his wallet and takes out the snapshot and looks at it ruefully.

CLOSE-UP—FELIX FRONT VIEW

Behind Felix in the distance, we see Riverside Drive and its old, tall apartment houses. Felix lowers his head into his hand to fight back the welling up of tears. The CAMERA PANS up past Felix and centers on the tall apartment house behind him.

The titles are finished.

The CAMERA continues upward and closer to the building. We center on a window, on the corner on the twelfth floor.

We are now directly outside the window, looking into the apartment. We MOVE IN.

INT. OSCAR'S APARTMENT—NIGHT

We see a smoke-filled room and a poker game in progress. The room is a complete mess. Dirty dishes, newspapers, beer cans (opened and unopened), laundry, ties, cigarette butts, spilled ashtrays, half-eaten sandwiches and fruit cores abound everywhere. There is an old-fashioned air conditioner in one of the windows that doesn't work and an old electric fan near the poker table that does. At the poker table there are six chairs, but only four men are sitting. One is MURRAY, who is doing something with the cards that resembles shuffling. The other players are ROY, SPEED and VINNIE. Vinnie has the largest stack of chips in front of him.

In the first full establishing LONG SHOT, we see all the players watching Murray as he goes through his interminable ritual of trying to shuffle the cards. Speed puffs hostilely on a cigar. Roy is wiping his sweating brow. The only sound we hear is the whirring of the electric fan.

The CAMERA MOVES IN closer and closer to Murray's face. His tongue sticks out of the side of his mouth as he is trying vainly to shuffle. The CAMERA PANS DOWN and we see his hands clumsily at work.

CLOSE-UP—SPEED

He watches Murray, puffing his cigar.

CLOSE-UP—VINNIE

He watches Murray, stacking his chips.

CLOSE-UP—ROY

He watches Murray, sweating.

FULL SHOT OF GROUP

SPEED
. . . Excuse me, sir, but aren't you the one they call the Cincinnati Kid?

MURRAY
(Still struggling with cards)
You don't like it, get a machine.

Speed turns angrily, he blows smoke from cigar. Mostly it goes in Roy's face.

ROY
Geez, it stinks in here.

Vinnie is measuring his chips.

VINNIE
(Looks at his watch)
What time is it?

CLOSE-UP—SPEED

SPEED
(Angrily turns to Vinnie)
Again what time is it?

FULL SHOT OF TABLE

VINNIE
My watch is slow, I'd like to know what time it is.

SPEED
You're winning ninety-five dollars, that's what time it is. Where the hell are you running?

VINNIE
I'm not running anywhere. I just asked what time it was.

ROY
(Looks at his watch)
It's ten-thirty.

There is a pause. Murray continues to shuffle.

VINNIE
I got to leave by twelve.

SPEED
(Turns in disgust)
Oh, Geez!

CLOSE-UP—VINNIE

VINNIE
I told you that when I sat down. I got to leave by twelve. Murray, didn't I say that when I sat down? I said I got to leave by twelve.

TWO SHOT—SPEED AND MURRAY

Murray starts dealing.

SPEED
All right, don't talk to him, he's dealing.
(To Murray)
Murray, you wanna rest for a while? Go lie down, sweetheart.

MURRAY

You want speed or accuracy, make up your mind.

He begins to deal slowly. Speed puffs on his cigar.

FULL SHOT—POKER GAME

ROY
(To Speed)
Hey, you wanna do me a really big favor? Smoke towards New Jersey.

Speed purposely blows smoke in his face. Roy blows smoke away with his hand and gets up and crosses to electric fan.

MURRAY

No kidding. I'm really worried about Felix. He's never been this late before.
Maybe somebody should call.
(Yells toward kitchen)
Hey, Oscar, why don't you call Felix?

CLOSE-UP—ROY

He's standing next to electric fan. He holds shirt collar open so the cool air will go inside.

ROY

Listen, why don't we chip in three dollars a piece and buy another window.
How the hell can you breathe in here.

CLOSE-UP—MURRAY

Dealing out cards, methodically.

MURRAY

How many cards you got, four?

SPEED

Yes, Murray, we all have four cards. When you give us one more, we'll all have five. If you gave us two more, we'd all have six. Understand how it works now?

MURRAY

Is Oscar playing or not? Hey, Oscar!

INT. KITCHEN—NIGHT

It's as messy as living room. No, worse. We see a refrigerator door open and a man's behind sticking out. He wears chino slacks and dirty sneakers. The man is humming gaily as he rummages through refrigerator. He stands up and we see it's OSCAR MADISON, about forty-three, sloppy and genial. He wears a sweaty half-sleeve polo shirt and a New York Mets baseball cap. He has two sandwiches in one hand and two cans of beer in the other. He puts beer under his arm and reaches into refrigerator again.

INT. REFRIGERATOR

It is an unholy mess. Most of the things are uncovered, a half-eaten lamb chop, bottles without caps, melting ice cream in a dish, etc. Oscar's hand reaches in to get a bottle of Coke and he knocks over a jar of syrup that drips onto the next shelf, getting the lamb chop. It's too horrible to describe. Oscar gets the Coke out.

CLOSE-UP—OSCAR

He now has the sandwiches and drinks and as he kicks the refrigerator door closed, he drops the sandwich on the floor.

MURRAY'S VOICE

Hey, Oscar, are you in or out?

Oscar reaches down to the floor, picks up the sandwich and wipes it off on his shirt.

OSCAR
(Calls out)
Out, pussycat, out!

He blows dirt off the sandwich.

POKER GAME IN LIVING ROOM—FULL SHOT

VINNIE
I told my wife I'd be home by one the latest. We're making an eight o'clock
plane to Florida. I told you that when I sat down.

*Roy gets up, throws in cards, wiping his neck with his handkerchief. He crosses to air
conditioner in window.*

ROY
Why doesn't he fix the air conditioner? It's ninety-eight degrees and it sits
there sweating like everyone else.

He bangs the air conditioner angrily with his fist.

MURRAY
Who goes to Florida in July?

CLOSE-UP—VINNIE

VINNIE
It's off season. There's no crowds and you get the best room for one tenth the
price. No cards.

CLOSE-UP—SPEED

SPEED
Some vacation. Six cheap people in an empty hotel.

CLOSE-UP—MURRAY

MURRAY

Dealer takes four . . . Hey, you think maybe Felix is sick. I mean he's never been this late before.

CLOSE-UP—ROY

He is walking around the room, mopping his brow and looking disgustedly at the trash around the room.

ROY

You know this is the same garbage from last week's game. I'm beginning to recognize things.

THREE SHOT OF MURRAY, SPEED AND VINNIE

MURRAY
(Throws cards in)
I'm out.

SPEED
(Shows hand, smiles)
Two kings.

VINNIE
Straight.

He shows hand, takes in pot. Speed glares at him.

MURRAY

Hey, maybe he's in his office locked in the john again. Did you know Felix was once locked in the john overnight? He wrote out his entire will on a half a roll of toilet paper. Heeee, what a nut!

Speed starts to shuffle and Vinnie starts to stack his chips.

SPEED

Don't play with your chips. I'm asking you nice. Don't play with your chips.

VINNIE

I'm not playing. I'm counting. Leave me alone, will you.

SPEED

I'll leave you alone if you stop playing with your chips.

He deals draw poker.

SPEED

I can't stand a guy who's winning who plays with his chips.

KITCHEN DOOR—POKER GAME—OSCAR'S LIVING ROOM—
NIGHT

Oscar comes out carrying tray of beer cans, sandwiches, peanuts and a bag of potato chips.

OSCAR

This is my house, Vinnie. You wanna play with your chips, you play with them, darling. I'm in for a quarter.

He crosses near table and sets the tray down on an easy chair.

CLOSE-UP—MURRAY

MURRAY

Aren't you gonna look at your cards first?

CLOSE-UP—OSCAR

OSCAR

What for? I'm gonna bluff anyway. Who gets the Pepsi?
(He opens a bottle of Pepsi)

FULL SHOT OF GAME

MURRAY
I get the Pepsi.

OSCAR
My friend Murray the policeman gets a warm Pepsi.
(He gives him bottle)

ROY
(Throws in some chips)
You still didn't fix the refrigerator? It's been two weeks now. No wonder it stinks in here.

OSCAR
(Picks up his cards and looks)
Temper, temper. If I wanted nagging I'd go back with my wife.
(Throws cards down)
I'm out. Who wants food?

MURRAY
What have you got?

OSCAR
(Looks under the bread)
I got brown sandwiches and green sandwiches.

CLOSE-UP—ROY
He grimaces in disgust.

CLOSE-UP—OSCAR

OSCAR
Which one do you want?

CLOSE-UP—MURRAY

MURRAY
What's the green?

CLOSE-UP—OSCAR

OSCAR
(Looks again)
It's either very new cheese or very old meat.

CLOSE-UP—MURRAY

MURRAY
I'll take the brown.

FULL SHOT OF GROUP

Oscar hands sandwich to Murray.

ROY
(Glares at Murray)
Are you crazy? You're not going to eat that, are you?

MURRAY
I'm hungry.

ROY
His refrigerator's been broken for two weeks. I saw milk standing in there that wasn't even in the bottle.

CLOSE-UP—OSCAR

OSCAR
What are you, some kind of health nut? Eat, Murray, eat.

FULL SHOT OF GAME

ROY
(Throws cards in)
I got six cards.

SPEED
That figures. I got three aces.

VINNIE
(Smiles)
Misdeal.

They all throw in cards. Speed begins to shuffle.

VINNIE
You know who makes good sandwiches? Felix. Did you ever taste his cream cheese and pimento on date nut bread?

SPEED
All right, make up your mind, poker or recipes.

He deals. Oscar is on his hands and knees beside the table, trying to open a can of beer with opener. He opens it and sprays a geyser of beer all over the table and the players. There is a hubbub as they all yell at Oscar derisively. They start to wipe themselves off and clean off the table and cards. Oscar hands Roy the overflowing can of beer.

OSCAR ON FLOOR

He lifts up the skirt of the slipcover on the chair and pushes the puddle of beer under the chair.

FULL SHOT OF GAME

The players begin to sit again as Oscar takes another can of beer and opens it. Again it sprays a geyser of liquid suds all over the players and table. They scream at Oscar as Murray tries to mop up the table with a towel that was hanging from the lamp near him.

OSCAR ON FLOOR

There is another puddle of beer on floor so Oscar takes the bread from the sandwiches and blots up the beer. Then he tosses the bread back on the tray. His hands are now wet so he dries them on Roy's coatsleeve, which is draped over Roy's chair.

FULL SHOT OF GAME

The other players are now all seated.

SPEED
Hey, Vinnie. Tell Oscar what time you're leaving.

VINNIE
(A trained dog)
Twelve o'clock.

SPEED
(To others)
You hear? We got ten minutes before the next announcement . . . all right, this game is five card stud. . . .
(He deals)
A red lady. . . . Deuce. . . . Quatro. . . . A big ace for the policeman.

CLOSE-UP—OSCAR

Who sits.

OSCAR
(Looks over table)
The pot's shy. Who didn't put in a quarter?

FULL SHOT OF GAME

MURRAY
You didn't.

OSCAR
You got a big mouth, Murray. Lend me twenty dollars, big mouth.

MURRAY
I just *loaned* you twenty dollars.

Speed is dealing another hand.

MURRAY
Borrow from somebody else. I keep winning my own money back.

They all join in a round of betting.

ROY
(To Oscar)
You owe everybody in the game. If you don't have it, you shouldn't play.

OSCAR
All right, I'm through being the nice one. You owe me six dollars apiece for the buffet.

SPEED
Buffet?
(They all react)
Hot beer and two sandwiches left over from when you went to high school?

THREE SHOT—MURRAY, VINNIE AND OSCAR

OSCAR
What do you want at a poker game, a tomato surprise? Murray, lend me twenty dollars or I'll call your wife and tell her you're in Central Park wearing a dress.

The phone rings.

MURRAY
Hey, maybe that's Felix.

Oscar gets up. Speed lays down his cards. Oscar crosses to phone.

SPEED
Pair of sixes . . .

VINNIE
Three deuces.

He reaches for money.

SPEED
(Angrily)
Why didn't you go to Florida last night?

CLOSE-UP—OSCAR

He picks up the phone.

OSCAR
Hello! Oscar the Poker Player!

PLAYERS AT TABLE

VINNIE
(Stacking chips)
If it's my wife, tell her I'm leaving at twelve.

SPEED
(Threatens with cigar)
You look at your watch once more, you get the peanuts in your face.
(To Roy)
Deal the cards!

CLOSE-UP—OSCAR

He gets comfortable on the sofa.

OSCAR
(Into phone)
Who? Who did you want, please? Dabby? ... Dabby who? ... No, there's no
Dabby here. ... Oh, *Daddy!*
(To others)
... For cryin' out loud, it's my kid.
(He smiles at players)

MED. SHOT: PLAYERS

Roy looks at him and shakes his head with disapproval. How can a man not recog-
nize his own child's voice.

CLOSE-UP—OSCAR

From this angle we see card game in B.G. (background).

> **OSCAR**
> *(Into phone. With great love)*
> Hya Brucey, baby, how are you?

There is a general outburst of AD-LIBBING from the poker players. Oscar turns to them angrily.

> **OSCAR**
> Hey, come on, give me a break, will ya. My five-year-old kid is calling from California. It must be costing him a fortune.
> *(Back into phone)*
> How've you been, sweetheart? Yes, I finally got your letter. It took three weeks. Next time you tell Mommy to give you a stamp. . . . I know, but you're not supposed to draw it on.

He laughs like a doting father. He turns proudly to the others.

> **OSCAR**
> You hear?

CLOSE-UP—SPEED

> **SPEED**
> *(Bored to death)*
> We hear. We hear. We're all thrilled.

CLOSE-UP—OSCAR—POKER TABLE IN B.G.

> **OSCAR**
> Mommy wants to speak to me? All right. Take care of yourself soldier. I love you.

VINNIE
(In b.g., dealing)
Ante a dollar.

SPEED
(Turns)
Cost you a dollar to play, Oscar. You got a dollar?

OSCAR
Not after I get through talking to this lady.
(Turns into phone; phony sweet)
Hello, Blanche, how are you? . . . Yes, I have a pretty good idea why you're calling. I'm a week behind with the check, right? *Four* weeks? That's not possible. I keep a record of every check and I happen to know I'm only *three* weeks behind. . . .

SPEED
(To Roy after looking at his hand)
What the hell kind of cards are you dealing here?

OSCAR
(Winces, then into phone)
All right, Blanche, don't threaten me with jail because it's not a threat. With my expenses and my alimony, a prisoner takes home more pay than I do. . . . Very nice language in front of children. . . .
(He winces as Blanche evidently has slammed down the phone. Oscar gets up and heads for poker table)
I'm eight hundred dollars behind in alimony so let's raise the stakes.

Oscar picks up his drink from poker table.

CLOSE-UP—ROY

ROY
She can do it, you know.

CLOSE-UP—OSCAR—WHO WALKS TO WINDOW

OSCAR
Do what?

ROY (VOICE)

Throw you in jail. For nonsupport of the kids.

OSCAR

Roy? They're living in their grandfather's house with a swimming pool in California. Poland could live for a year on what my kids leave over for lunch. Can we play cards?

CLOSE-UP—ROY

ROY

I told you you would get into trouble. It's because you don't know how to manage anything. I should know. I'm your accountant.
(*He picks up bag of potato chips*)

MED. SHOT—OSCAR COMES TO ROY

OSCAR

If you're my accountant, how come I need money?

ROY

If you need money, how come you play poker?

OSCAR

Because I need money.

ROY

But you always lose.

OSCAR

That's why I need the money.

ROY

(*Heated*)
Then don't play poker.

OSCAR

Then don't come to my house and eat my potato chips.

FULL SHOT—GROUP AT POKER TABLE

Oscar has put down his drink and tries to grab the bag of potato chips away from Roy. Roy struggles with him and the bag breaks showering the table and everyone with potato chips. Everyone ad-libs yelling.

MURRAY
What are you yelling about? We're playing a friendly game.

SPEED
Who's playing? We've been sitting here talking since eight o'clock.

VINNIE
Since seven. That's why I said I was going to quit at twelve.

SPEED
(Picks up a banana and threatens him)
How'd you like a stale banana right in the mouth?

There is a general shouting until Murray quiets them all.

MURRAY
All right, all right, let's calm down. Take it easy. I'm a cop you know, I could arrest the whole lousy game.

They all sit quietly.

CLOSE-UP—OSCAR

OSCAR
My friend Murray the cop is right. Let's just play cards. And please hold them up, I can't see where I marked them.

The phone rings. Oscar gets up, crosses to phone.

CLOSE-UP—ROY

ROY
(To the others)
He owes money to his wife, his government and his friends and he still won't
take it seriously.

CLOSE-UP—OSCAR

He picks up phone.

OSCAR
(To Roy)
Life goes on even for those of us who are divorced, broke and sloppy. Hello.
(Into phone)
Divorced, Broke and Sloppy. . . . Oh, hello, sweetheart.
*(He becomes seductive. He pulls phone to side and talks low, but others can still
hear)*
I told you not to call me during the game. I can't talk to you now.

FULL SHOT—TABLE

*Murray winks at Vinnie and shoves his elbow as if to say, "What an operator." They
all watch, enjoying it.*

CUT BACK TO:

OSCAR—ON PHONE

OSCAR
You know I do, dear . . .
(He kisses into phone)
All right, just a minute.
(He turns to table)
Murray, it's your wife.

INT. OSCAR'S LIVING ROOM—FULL SHOT—NIGHT

Murray looks at the others sheepishly and then gets up and crosses to phone. Oscar hands it to him and sits on sofa.

MURRAY
(Hand over phone)
I wish you *were* having an affair with her. Then she wouldn't bother me all the time.
(Into phone)
Hello, Mimi, what's wrong?

OSCAR
(Mimics Mimi)
What time are you coming home?
(Mimics Murray)
I don't know, about twelve, twelve-thirty.

MURRAY
(Into phone) '
I don't know. About twelve, twelve-thirty.

In b.g., Speed gets up, yawns and goes to bathroom.

MURRAY
(Into phone)
Why, what did you want, Mimi? . . . A corned beef sandwich and a strawberry malted?

OSCAR
Is she pregnant again?

MURRAY
(Hand over phone)
No, just fat.
(Into phone)
. . . What? . . . How could you hear that? I had the phone over my chest.

EXT. BATHROOM DOOR

We hear a flush and Speed comes out as Vinnie goes in.

TWO SHOT—OSCAR AND MURRAY

MURRAY
(Into phone)
Who? . . . Felix? . . . No, he didn't show up tonight. What's
wrong? . . . You're kidding. . . . How should I know? . . . All right, Mimi, I'll
take care of it. Goodbye.
(He hangs up)
What did I tell you? Felix is missing.

LONG SHOT OF ROOM—INCLUDING ALL

SPEED
What do you mean, missing?

MURRAY
He didn't show up for work today. He didn't come home tonight. No one
knows where he is. Mimi just spoke to his wife.

OSCAR
Wait a minute. No one is missing for one day.

TWO SHOT—ROY, OSCAR

Roy sitting in armchair. Oscar paces behind him puffing his cigar.

ROY
Maybe he had an accident.

OSCAR
They would have heard.

ROY
If he's laying in a gutter somewhere, who would know who he is?

OSCAR

He's got ninety-two credit cards in his wallet. The minute something happens to him America lights up. . . . I'll call his wife.

FULL SHOT OF ROOM

Oscar picks up phone.

TWO SHOT—VINNIE AND SPEED

Vinnie is sitting while Speed paces nervously behind him.

VINNIE
(To Speed)
I thought he looked edgy the last couple of weeks. Didn't you think he looked edgy?

SPEED
(With hostility)
No, as a matter of fact, I thought *you* looked edgy.

CLOSE-UP—OSCAR, MURRAY AND ROY IN BACKGROUND

He is seated on sofa, phone in hand. Murray and Roy hover over him and behind him.

OSCAR
(Into phone)
Hello, Frances. Oscar. I just heard.

ROY
Tell her not to worry. She's probably hysterical.

MURRAY
Yeah, you know women.

OSCAR

Listen, Frances, the most important thing is not to worry . . . OH!

(Turns to others)

She's not worried.

MURRAY

Sure.

OSCAR

(Into phone)

Frances, do you have any idea where he could be? He what? You're kidding? Why? No, I didn't know. . . . Gee, that's too bad. All right, listen, Frances, you just sit tight and the minute I hear anything I'll let you know. Goodbye.

(He hangs up. He sits a minute thinking, then gets up)

FULL SHOT OF GROUP

Oscar walks away from sofa, puffing on cigar, deep in thought. They all wait anxiously for some word. They can't wait any longer.

MURRAY

Ya gonna tell us or do we hire a private detective?

OSCAR

They broke up.

ROY

Who?

OSCAR

(He looks at Roy as though he's a cretin)

Felix and Frances. They broke up. The entire marriage is through.

VINNIE

You're kidding.

SPEED

After twelve years?

Oscar sits down at table.

VINNIE

They were such a happy couple.

MURRAY

He'll go to pieces. I know Felix. He's gonna try something crazy.

SPEED

That's all he ever used to talk about, his wife and his kids.

MURRAY

He'll kill himself. You hear what I'm saying. He's gonna go out and try to kill himself.

SPEED

(Shouts at Murray)

Will you shut up, Murray. Stop being a cop for two minutes.

(Softly to Oscar)

Where'd he go, Oscar?

OSCAR

He went out to kill himself.

MURRAY

What did I tell you?

ROY

(To Oscar)

Are you serious?

OSCAR

That's what she said. He was going out to kill himself. He didn't want to do it at home 'cause the kids were sleeping.

VINNIE

Why?

OSCAR

Why? Because Felix is a nut, that's why.

VINNIE

But is that what he said? In those words? "I'm going out to kill myself"?

OSCAR

I don't know in what words. She didn't read it to me.

ROY

You mean he left her a note?

OSCAR

No. He sent a telegram.

MURRAY

. . . A suicide telegram? Who sends a suicide telegram?

OSCAR

Felix, the nut, that's who. Can you imagine getting a thing like that? She even has to tip the kid a quarter.

EXT. ELEVATOR DOOR ON OSCAR'S LANDING—NIGHT

The self-service door opens and we see Felix standing in the elevator. He is leaning up against the back of the elevator, one hand covering his eyes, a dejected, beaten man. It is a moment before he realizes the door has opened. He looks up and sees that he's arrived on his floor. He starts out just as the elevator door closes. The door bangs up against his arm and Felix, as only Felix can, winces in terrible pain and holds his arm as he steps out on the floor.

INT. OSCAR'S APARTMENT—FULL SHOT OF GROUP—NIGHT

MURRAY

Maybe he's just bluffing. We get these cases every day. All they want is a little sympathy. We got a guy who calls us every Saturday afternoon from the George Washington Bridge.

ROY

I don't know. You never can tell what a guy will do when he's hysterical.

MURRAY

Nahhh. Nine times out of ten they don't jump.

ROY
What about the tenth time?

MURRAY
They jump. He's right. There's a possibility.

OSCAR
Not with Felix. I know him. He's too nervous to kill himself. He wears his
seat belt in a drive-in movie.

VINNIE
Isn't there someplace we could look for him?

SPEED
Where? Where would you look? Who knows where he is?

The doorbell rings. They all freeze.

OSCAR
Of course. If you're gonna kill yourself, where's the safest place to do it?
With your friends.

Vinnie starts for the door.

MURRAY
(Stops him)
Wait a minute. The guy may be hysterical. Let's play it nice and easy. If we're
calm, maybe he'll be calm.

ROY
(Joining them)
That's right. That's how they do it with those guys out on the ledge. You talk
nice and soft.

INT. HALL—OSCAR'S LANDING

Felix is at door and rings bell again. He rubs his eyes with hand, oh the grief and woe.

FULL GROUP IN ROOM

SPEED
(Joins group)
What'll we say to him?

MURRAY
We don't say nothin'. Like we never heard a thing.

OSCAR
(Who's been watching this)
You through with this discussion? 'Cause he already could have hung himself out in the hall. Vinnie, open the door.

MURRAY
Remember, like we don't know nothin'.

They all rush back to their seats and grab up cards, which they concentrate on with great intensity.

INT. OSCAR'S APARTMENT AT DOOR

Vinnie looks to see if they're all settled, then opens the door. Felix enters, hands in pockets again.

VINNIE
Hi, Felix. . . .

FELIX
Hi, Vin. . . .
(Looks into room)
Hi, Fellas.

GROUP AT TABLE

They all look up and feint surprise and try to act nonchalant as they mumble "hello" and then resume concentration on the game. Vinnie rejoins them.

CLOSE-UP—FELIX

He takes his coat off, folds it neatly and lays it on chair. He smooths it down.

FELIX
How's the game goin'?

FULL SHOT—TABLE

They barely look up and mumble, "Fine, fine." They glance at each other.

MEDIUM SHOT—FELIX

FELIX
Good. Good. . . . Sorry, I'm late.

He crosses to chair where the sandwiches Oscar made are resting. He picks up the bread, and looks in it and grimaces in disgust and tosses bread back on tray. Felix looks over the filthy empty bottles in the room.

FELIX
Any ginger ale left?

TABLE

Oscar looks up.

OSCAR
Ginger ale? Gee, I don't think so, Fel. I got some root beer.

CLOSE-UP—FELIX

FELIX
No, I felt like a ginger ale. I just don't feel like a root beer . . . tonight.

He says this last as if they should get his hidden meaning, whatever that may be.

FULL SHOT—TABLE

Felix crosses and watches the game.

OSCAR
What's the bet?

SPEED
You bet a quarter. It's up to Murray. Murray, what do you say?

Murray is staring at Felix.

SPEED
Murray! . . . Murray!

ROY
Tap his shoulder.

VINNIE
(Taps Murray's shoulder)
Murray!

MURRAY
(Jumps, startled)
What? What?

SPEED
It's up to you.

MURRAY
Why is it always up to me?

SPEED
It's not always up to you. It's up to you now. What do you do?

MURRAY
I'm in. I'm in.
(He throws in a quarter)

FELIX
(Watching cards)
Er . . . anyone call about me?

OSCAR
Not that I can remember. . . . Did anyone call for Felix?
(They all ad-lib "No")
Why, were you expecting a call?

FELIX
No, no. Just asking.

He turns. Hanging from the book shelf is a toy airplane, Brucey's. Felix pathetically spins the propeller.

ROY
Raise a dollar.

SPEED
Costs me a dollar and a quarter then, right?

OSCAR
Right.

FELIX
(Still playing with plane)
I just thought someone might have called.

SPEED
(Nervously)
What does it cost me to play again?

MURRAY
(Angry)
A dollar and a quarter! A dollar and a quarter! Pay attention for God's sake.

ROY
All right, take it easy. Take it easy.

OSCAR

Let's calm down, everyone, heh?

MURRAY

I'm sorry. I can't help it.
(Points to Speed)
He makes me nervous.

SPEED

I make *you* nervous? You make *me* nervous. You make everyone nervous.

MURRAY

(Sarcastic)
I'm sorry. Forgive me. I'll kill myself.

OSCAR

Murray!
(He motions with his head to Felix)

MURRAY

Oh, sorry.

They all glare at Murray.

MEDIUM SHOT—FELIX

He wanders over to the open window and looks out across to New Jersey's Palisades all lit up.

FELIX

Gee, it's a pretty view from here. What is it, twelve floors?

OSCAR

He quickly gets up from table and rushes to window.

OSCAR

No, no. It's only eleven. It says twelve but it's really only eleven.

Oscar closes the window, then shivers.

OSCAR

It's chilly in here. Isn't it chilly in here?
He crosses back to table.

FULL SHOT—TABLE

They all close the windows. Oscar sits.

OSCAR

Want to sit down and play, Fel? It's still early.

VINNIE

Sure. We're in no rush. We'll be here till three, four in the morning.

Speed glares at Vinnie.

CLOSE-UP—FELIX AT WINDOW

FELIX

I don't know. I just don't feel much like playing now.

He crosses past the table.

OSCAR

Where are you going?

FELIX

To the john.

CLOSE-UP—OSCAR

OSCAR
(Looks at players)
Alone?

CLOSE-UP—FELIX

who stops at door of john, puzzled.

FELIX
I always go alone. . . . Why?

CLOSE-UP—OSCAR

OSCAR
No reason. . . . You gonna be in there long?

CLOSE-UP—FELIX

As long as it takes.

He goes into bathroom and shuts door behind him.

FULL SHOT—GROUP

The minute he's gone, the players jump up and crowd about the bathroom door, whispering in frenzied anxiety.

MURRAY
Are you crazy, letting him go to the john alone?

ROY
Suppose he tries to kill himself?

OSCAR
How's he gonna kill himself in the john?

MURRAY

What do you mean, how? Razor blades, poison, anything that's in there.

OSCAR

That's the kids' bathroom. The worst he could do is brush his teeth to death.

ROY

He could jump.

VINNIE

That's right. Isn't there a window in there?

OSCAR

It's only six inches wide.

MURRAY

He could break the glass. He could cut his wrists.

OSCAR

He could also flush himself into the East River. I tell you he's not gonna try anything.
(He moves away from door)

ROY

Shh!
(He puts his head to door)
Listen! . . . He's crying.

From inside we hear Felix begin to sob.

ROY

You hear that. He's crying.

MURRAY

Isn't that terrible? For God's sake, Oscar, do something. Say something.

OSCAR

What? What do you say to a man who's crying in your bathroom?

There is the sound of the toilet flushing.

ROY
He's coming!

They all scramble quickly back to their places at the table. Murray and Vinnie get mixed up and sit in the wrong chairs but quickly straighten it out just as Felix comes back in the room. He seems calm and collected but makes a straight line for the door.

FELIX
I guess I'll be running along.

They all jump up in a loud hubbub in an effort to stop him. They mustn't let him out of their sight.

OSCAR
Felix, wait a second.

FELIX
No, no. I can't talk to you. I can't talk to anyone.

They all try to grab him and stop him at the stairs.

MURRAY
Felix, we're your friends. Don't run out like this.

FELIX
(Struggles to pull away)
No, fellows, no.

OSCAR
Felix, sit down a minute. Talk to us.

FELIX
There's nothing to talk over. There's nothing to say. It's over. Let me go, will you.

He breaks out of their grip and runs inside down the hall toward the bedrooms.
    Felix darts into a room and the others chase after him. Oscar watches all this from the hall. Another door opens and Felix emerges and runs farther down the hall.

FELIX
Leave me alone, fellas, please.

The other players emerge from the room and chase after Felix down the hall. He rushes into the master bedroom.

MURRAY
Stop him! Stop him!

VINNIE
Don't let him get to the bedroom!

They arrive at the bedroom door just as Felix closes it in their faces.

INT. MASTER BEDROOM

It was once a nice room like the rest of the house, but like the rest under Oscar's slovenliness, it has gone to pot.

FELIX
(Holding back door and almost sobbing again)
I don't want to talk about it, fellas, leave me alone.

INT. HALL OUTSIDE DOOR

They're all pushing on the door. Oscar joins them.

OSCAR
Go ahead. Break it down!

They all give it a mighty heave and the door gives.

FELIX ON OTHER SIDE

He is holding back door when suddenly their combined strength swings it open full force. Felix is hurled flat up against the wall behind the door.

The others rush into the room. They don't see Felix because he's still pinned behind the door.

MURRAY
(Looks around)
He jumped! My God, he jumped.

From behind the door we hear Felix.

FELIX
My back! My back!

SPEED
Get him! Get him!

Felix bent over, staggers to the bed.

FELIX
Fellas, please, leave me alone, I'm all right. Ohh, my stomach.
(He grabs his stomach)

MURRAY
What's the matter with your stomach?

FELIX
Nothing. Nothing's the matter with my stomach. I didn't take anything.
Leave me alone. Ohh.

He grimaces in pain. They hover over him as he lays on the bed.

OSCAR
What do you mean you didn't take anything? What did you take?

FELIX

Nothing! Nothing! I didn't take anything. Don't tell Frances what I did, please.

VINNIE

No, no . . .

OSCAR

He took pills.

MURRAY

How many pills?

OSCAR

What kind of pills?

FELIX

I didn't take any pills. I don't know what kind they were. Little green ones. I just grabbed anything out of her medicine cabinet. I must have been crazy.
(Grabs Vinnie's arm)
Don't call her. Don't call Frances.

VINNIE

I won't call her.

OSCAR

When did you take them?

FELIX

I don't know. A couple of hours ago. I can't remember.
(Grabbing Vinnie)
You won't call Frances.

VINNIE

I won't call her.

OSCAR

How many pills did you take?

FELIX

I don't know. I can't remember. I think a whole bottle.

EVERYONE
(Practically screaming)
A whole bottle!

FELIX
(Grabs Vinnie)
You mustn't tell her, Vinnie.

VINNIE
(Smiles)
I won't say a word.

TWO SHOT—OSCAR AND MURRAY

OSCAR
You don't even know what kind.

MURRAY
What's the difference. He took a whole bottle.

OSCAR
Maybe they were vitamins. He could be the healthiest one in the room. Take it easy, will ya.

FULL SHOT—FELIX ON BED. MURRAY, ROY AND VINNIE ARE THROWN INTO A PANIC AS THEY LIFT HIM UP TO SAVE THEIR FRIEND'S LIFE

SPEED
Walk him around. Don't let him go to sleep.

FELIX
The back . . . watch the back!

MURRAY
Open his collar. Open the window. Give him some air.

They're walking him around the room.

ROY

Rub his wrists. Keep his circulation going.
(He begins to slap Felix in the face to wake him up)

FELIX

My back . . . my back.

VINNIE

A cold compress. Put a cold compress on his neck.

They are all administering to Felix as they walk him around the room. Oscar gets on the bed.

OSCAR

(Who surveys the scene with great disdain)
One doctor at a time, heh? All the interns shut the hell up.

FELIX

I'm all right, I'm all right.
(To Vinnie)
You didn't call Frances, did you?

MURRAY

The bathroom. Get his head under the cold shower.

SPEED

(Holding Felix on other side)
Vinnie, turn the shower on.

Vinnie runs into the bathroom as the four players drag Felix into the bathroom that adjoins Oscar's bedroom.

FELIX

My arm, my arm, you're hurting my arm.

BATHROOM—OSCAR'S APARTMENT—NIGHT

Vinnie reaches in and turns the shower on. The others drag the protesting Felix in and try to get his head under the shower.

FELIX

Let me go, I'm all right, please.

They force his head under and the cold shower pours on Felix's head.

MURRAY

We got to get the pills out.

FELIX

They're out. I threw up before. You didn't call Frances did ya?

The cold water continues to drench Felix's head as we

DISSOLVE:

THE LIVING ROOM—A FEW MINUTES LATER

Felix sits in the big chair in the center of the room, a big towel around his neck. They all sit and stand around him.

FELIX

Twelve years. Twelve years we were married. Did you know we were married twelve years, Roy?

ROY
(Comforting him)
Yes, Felix. I knew.

FELIX

And now it's over. Like that, it's over. That's hysterical, isn't it?

CLOSE-UP—SPEED

SPEED
Maybe it was just a fight. You've had fights before, Felix.

CLOSE-UP—FELIX

FELIX
No, it's over. She's getting a lawyer tomorrow. *My* cousin. She's using *my* cousin.
(*He sobs*)
Who am *I* going to get?

FULL SHOT—LIVING ROOM

Murray looks at others sadly, then goes to Felix and pats his shoulder.

MURRAY
It's okay, Felix.

Speed and Roy are standing on either side of Murray.

MURRAY (CONT'D)
All right, let's not stand around looking at him. Let's break it up, heh?

Murray pushes Speed and Roy hard like a cop breaking up a crowd.

FELIX

Still sobbing and has his head in his hands.

FELIX
Yes, don't stand there looking at me, fellas. I'm so ashamed.

OSCAR
Come on, he's all right. Let's call it a night.

TWO SHOT—FELIX AND VINNIE

VINNIE
It's all right, Felix. We understand.

FELIX
(Grabs Vinnie)
Hey, Vinnie don't say anything about this to anyone. Will you promise me?

VINNIE
I'm going to Florida tomorrow.

FELIX
(Trying to be brave and cheerful)
Oh, that's nice. Have a good time.

VINNIE
Thanks.

FELIX
(Turns away and sighs)
We were going to Florida next winter. Without the kids.
(Laughs, then sobs)
Now they'll go without me!

FULL SHOT—LIVING ROOM

Oscar ushers them all to door as they grab their coats.

OSCAR
All right, come on.

They are all grouped on the one step-up landing near the door. They speak softly as Felix is still sobbing and they don't want him to hear them.

MURRAY
Maybe one of us should stay.

OSCAR
It's all right, Murray.

MURRAY
Suppose he tries something again.

OSCAR
He won't try anything again.

MURRAY
How do you know he won't try anything again?

CLOSE-UP—FELIX

FELIX
I won't try anything again. I'm very tired.
(*He hears only what he wants to hear*)

GROUP AT DOOR

OSCAR
You hear? He's very tired. He had a busy night. Goodnight, fellows.

They all ad-lib good-byes and leave. Oscar turns his back to door when suddenly it opens again and Roy takes one step in.

ROY
If anything happens, Oscar, just call me.

He exits and as the door starts to close, it reopens and Speed comes in.

SPEED
I'm three blocks away. I could be here in five minutes.

He exits and as the door starts to close, it reopens and Vinnie comes back in.

VINNIE
If you need me, I'll be at the Meridian Motel in Miami Beach.

OSCAR
You'll be the first one I'll call, Vinnie.

Vinnie exits. The door closes and then reopens as Murray comes back.

MURRAY
(To Oscar)
You sure?

OSCAR
I'm sure.

ANGLE INCLUDING FELIX IN B.G.

MURRAY
(Loud, false cheeriness)
Goodnight, Felix. Try to get a good night's sleep. I guarantee you things are going to look a lot brighter in the morning.

CLOSE SHOT—MURRAY AND OSCAR

MURRAY
(Whisper)
Take away his belt and his shoelaces.

Oscar nods and gently pushes Murray out, who closes the door.

LONG SHOT OF FELIX, HEAD DEJECTED IN HIS LAP, AND OSCAR ON THE LANDING

He gives a long look at Felix. There is a pause.

OSCAR
(Sighs)
Ohh, Felix, Felix, Felix, Felix!

FELIX
(He sits with his head in his hands, doesn't look up)
I know, I know, I know, I know. . . . Oscar, what am I going to do?

OSCAR
We'll talk about it. But first we'll have something to eat. I'll make you some Ovaltine. You like hot Ovaltine?

FELIX
Oscar, the terrible thing is, I still love her. You know I've always loved her, Oscar.

OSCAR
You want some vanilla wafers or Vienna fingers? Animal crackers, I got everything. C'mon. . . .

FELIX
We had so much, Oscar. We had two beautiful kids, a beautiful home. Who had more beautiful kids or a more beautiful home than me, Oscar? Who?

OSCAR
Nobody.
(Looks into a jar)
You want some Ritz crackers with some peanut butter . . . or whatever this was.

FELIX
. . . Twelve years of marriage . . . down the drain.

INT. KITCHEN

Oscar enters. Felix follows. The sight of the kitchen almost makes Felix nauseous.

OSCAR
Drains can be fixed. That's why they have plumbers.
(Gets jar of Ovaltine)
Get me a pot under the sink.

FELIX
(Bending down under sink)
It's not fair, dammit, it's not fair.
(He reaches over and suddenly gets a spasm of pain)
Oooh! Ooh!
(He is bent over in the position of trying to get the pot. He becomes immobile.)

OSCAR
(Turns quickly)
What's the matter?

FELIX
My neck. My neck. I got a nerve spasm in the neck.

OSCAR
(Tries to help)
All right, take it easy. Show me where it hurts.

FELIX
I can't straighten up.
(Oscar starts to pull him)
Don't touch me! Don't touch me!

OSCAR
I just want to see where it hurts.

FELIX
(Quickly; yells)
No! No! ... It's tension. I get it from tension. I must be tense.

He finally straightens up, manages to sit on a kitchen chair.

OSCAR
I wouldn't be surprised.
(Gets behind Felix and starts to rub neck; he yells)
Relax, dammit, relax!

FELIX
(Yells back)
Don't yell at me ... Ooh! Ooh!

OSCAR
Does that hurt?

FELIX
No, it feels good.

OSCAR

Then say so. You make the same sound for pain or happiness.

FELIX

I know it. I know it, Oscar. I think I'm crazy.

OSCAR

Well, if it'll make you feel any better, I think so too.

FELIX

It doesn't take much, Oscar. The first sign of trouble, I go to pieces like that.
(He snaps fingers, grimaces)

OSCAR

You didn't hurt your fingers, did you?

FELIX

No, it feels good when you rub. Don't stop.

OSCAR
(Still rubbing)
If you don't relax, I'll break my hands.
(Touches Felix's hair)
Look at this. The only man in the world with clenched hair. Bend over. Now
take a deep breath . . . a deep breath.

*Felix bends way over and Oscar starts to massage his back thoroughly, pushing, rub-
bing, banging with sides of hands. It looks almost professional but he does it helter-
skelter all over his back.*

OSCAR
(Still massaging)
Listen, if this hurts just tell me because I don't know what the hell I'm doing.

Felix starts to wheeze.

OSCAR
What is that sound?

FELIX
(Rising)
I can't breathe. It's all the dust in this apartment. Let me open the window. I need some air.

OSCAR
We're not opening any windows on the eleventh floor. You want air, we'll get fresh air.
(He grabs Felix)
Come on, we'll take a walk. It'll do you good.

They both exit. Felix is wheezing. The kitchen door swings closed.

DISSOLVE:

EXT. BROADWAY IN THE EIGHTIES, ABOUT 11—NIGHT

Felix and Oscar walking along the street. Oscar has a dirty, rumpled seersucker jacket over his sweatshirt, sans baseball cap. He is licking an ice cream cone.

FELIX
I wish I were like you, Oscar. Strong. I'm weak. Oh, yes, I admit it. Weak. Weak weak weak weak.

OSCAR
You'll outlive today's entire generation . . . You want a lick?

FELIX
You don't understand, I'm nothing without my wife and kids. Nothing!!!

Oscar looks at Felix.

OSCAR
No, you're not nothing. You're *something!* A person. You're flesh and blood and bones and hair and nails and ears.
(He begins wagging ice cream cone at him)

You're not a fish. You're not a buffalo. You're *you!* You walk and talk and cry and complain and eat little green pills and send suicide telegrams. No one else does that Felix. I'm telling you, *you're the only one of its kind in the world!*

With this last gesticulation, the ice cream flies out of the cone and plops unappetizingly on Felix's lapel. He looks down at it in disgust.

OSCAR
Woops!

FELIX
(Taking ice cream off)
That's a stain. You stained me. Chocolate ice cream stains.

OSCAR
Ice cream doesn't stain.

FELIX
Vanilla and coffee doesn't stain. Chocolate stains. That's a stain.

He tries wiping it off with despair, as though this was also part of the giant plot to destroy Felix.

DISSOLVE:

INT. STARK'S RESTAURANT—BROADWAY IN THE EIGHTIES—NIGHT

Felix and Oscar are sitting opposite each other in a booth. Felix has a glass of water in front of him and is rubbing his stain desperately with a handkerchief, dipping it into the water. His lapel has a large wet blot. Oscar watches him with disdain.

OSCAR
Why don't you stop it, Felix? You're gonna get a water stain.

FELIX
(Still rubbing)
That's not going to come out. That's a permanent stain.

CLOSE-UP—WAITRESS

A large, HEAVY-SET BLONDE in her late thirties, but sexy.

WAITRESS
You ready to order now?

THREE SHOT—FELIX, OSCAR AND WAITRESS

Oscar gives a big smile when he sees girl.

OSCAR
Ahh, there's my pussycat. Come here, darling.
(He puts an arm around her waist; he bites her arm)
For a tip tonight, I'm gonna leave you the key to my apartment.

WAITRESS
Is it informal or can I bring my husband?

OSCAR
Never mind. I can't wait that long. How about five quick minutes behind the
cash register?
(He bites her arm again)

WAITRESS
(Holding pad and pencil)
If you bite, I can't write. What'll you have?

FELIX
(A little embarrassed)
A cup of hot tea for me, please.

OSCAR
A cup of hot tea for Diamond Jim Brady . . . and let's see, I just had an ice
cream . . . and I'll have a brisket of beef sandwich, all fat and high caloric
cream soda.

Oscar gives the waitress a little pat on the fanny as she goes. Oscar looks at Felix.

OSCAR

If you don't try, how're you gonna find out?

FELIX

(Seems chilly. Puts arms around himself)
Exactly. It's easy for you and me, Oscar. We're men. We're out in the world, we can meet new people. What about Frances?

OSCAR

(Picks teeth with toothpick)
What *about* Frances?

FELIX

Divorce is much harder on the woman, Oscar. She's all alone with the kids. Stuck there in the house. She can't get out like me. I mean where is she going to find someone now at her age? With two kids? Where?

OSCAR

I don't know. Maybe someone will come to the door. . . . Can we stop talking about Frances?

FELIX

What do you want me to do, Oscar, forget about her? How do you wipe out twelve years of marriage just like that?

OSCAR

Those are the facts, Felix. You've got to face it. You can't spend the rest of your life crying. It annoys people in the movies.
(He notices Felix rubbing himself)
What's the matter with you?

FELIX

I'm cold. It's the air-conditioning. Why do they always turn it up so high? I'll probably get the flu.

OSCAR

You want me to ask them for a blanket?

FELIX
(Shivers)
You've got to be very careful with air-conditioning. Frances and I have one in our bedroom but I never let her turn it on in the summer.

OSCAR
She must be crazy about that.

Felix looks up at blower, then picks up all his silverware, and Oscar's.

FELIX
Let's move to another table.

He moves to another table. Oscar follows him, without enthusiasm. Felix begins to set the other table with the silverware. Oscar looks at him with disdain.

CLOSER SHOT—FELIX

He has the table all set but suddenly begins to make queer humming sounds.

CLOSE-UP—OSCAR

worried.

OSCAR
What's the matter now?

CLOSE-UP—FELIX

FELIX
My ears are closing up. I have this sinus trouble. It's the change in temperature. I always get it with air-conditioning.

Felix begins to tilt head over, then bangs one ear, then reverses the process with the other ear.

CLOSE-UP—OSCAR

> **OSCAR**
> Maybe it'll go away.

CLOSE-UP—FELIX

> **FELIX**
> No, it's all part of my allergies. I get them in the summer.

He yawns trying to open ears.

TWO SHOT—OSCAR, FELIX

> **OSCAR**
> Only in the summer?

> **FELIX**
> *(Nods)*
> And in the winter. I get them all year. I'm allergic to foods, pillows, curtains, perfumes. Can you imagine that? Perfumes. It used to drive Frances crazy. For a while the only thing she could wear was my aftershave lotion. Oh, I was impossible to live with.

He tries to swallow hoping to open the ears that way. It's unsuccessful so he bellows loud, like a moose.

FULL SHOT—OTHER TABLES

The people look incredulously at Felix.

TWO SHOT—FELIX AND OSCAR

It takes a lot to embarrass someone like Oscar, but he is clearly embarrassed.

OSCAR

Stop that . . . what are you doing?

FELIX

I'm trying to clear my ears. You create a pressure inside your head and then the eustachian tubes open up.

(He bellows again)

FULL SHOT—PEOPLE IN ROOM

They look at Felix in bewilderment.

TWO SHOT—FELIX AND OSCAR

Felix gives one more loud bellow.

OSCAR

Did it open up?

FELIX

(Moves his head, testing it)
A little bit.
(He rubs his neck)
I think I strained my throat.

Oscar buries his head on his arm on the table.

DISSOLVE:

RIVERSIDE DRIVE—SOLDIERS AND SAILORS MONUMENT—NIGHT

Felix and Oscar are walking along the drive. A half hour later. Felix is rubbing his neck and clearing his throat.

OSCAR

Felix, why don't you leave yourself alone. Don't tinker.

FELIX

I know it. But I can't help myself, Oscar. I drive everyone crazy. A marriage counselor once kicked me out of his office. He wrote on my chart, "Lunatic"! . . .

They stop at a bench and Oscar stretches out on it full length.

OSCAR

It takes two to make a rotten marriage.

FELIX
(Paces back and forth in front of Oscar)
You don't know what I was like at home. I'm a compulsive cleaner. I'm always cleaning up after Frances. . . . Then I go in the kitchen and recook all her meals, because I'm also a better cook. Weell, I cooked myself right out of a marriage.

TWO SHOT—FELIX, OSCAR

Felix sits on the end of the bench and bangs his head with the palm of his hand three times.

FELIX

. . . Stupid—damned-idiot!

OSCAR

Hey, don't do that. You'll get a headache.

FELIX

I can't stand it, Oscar. I hate me. Oh, boy, do I hate me.

OSCAR
(Still reclining)
You don't hate you. You love you. You think no one else has problems like you.

FELIX
(Hurt)
I thought you were my friend.

OSCAR
That's why I can talk to you like this. Because I love you almost as much as you do . . .

FELIX
Then help me, Oscar.

OSCAR
How can I help you when I can't help myself?
(Oscar sits up)
You think *you're* impossible to live with? Blanche used to say, "What time do you want dinner?" And I'd say, "I don't know. I'm not hungry." Then at three o'clock in the morning I'd wake her up and say, "Now"! . . . I've been one of the highest paid sportswriters in the east for the past fourteen years and we saved eight and a half dollars—in pennies. I'm never home, I gamble, I burn cigar holes in the furniture, drink like a fish and lie to her every chance I get. And for our tenth wedding anniversary, I took her to see the New York Rangers–Detroit Red Wings hockey game . . . where she got hit by a puck. And I still can't understand why she left me. That's how impossible I am.
(He gets up)
Come on, it's late. The muggers'll be here soon.

They walk off. They start to cross the street toward Oscar's house. The CAMERA stays on their backs. We hear them talking as they walk.

FELIX
I don't think I can take it living alone, Oscar. In two weeks I'll go to pieces. How will I work? How will I make a living?

OSCAR
You'll go on street corners and cry. They'll throw nickels at you. You'll work, Felix, you'll work.

As they walk, Felix spots a piece of newspaper floating around near the ground. In-stinctively, he picks it up and puts it in the trash can. Oscar pulls him along and they cross the street.

DISSOLVE:

EXT. ELEVATOR DOOR ON OSCAR'S LANDING—NIGHT

The door opens and Felix and Oscar step out.

OSCAR

. . . So tonight you're going to sleep here. And tomorrow you're going to get your clothes and your electric toothbrush and you'll move in with me.

We follow them down the hall.

FELIX

No, no. It's your apartment. I'll be in the way.

OSCAR

There's eight rooms. We could go for a year without seeing each other. Don't you understand? I *want* you to move in.

FELIX

Why? I'm a pest.

OSCAR

I know you're a pest. You don't have to keep telling me.

They stop at Oscar's door.

FELIX

Then why do you want me to live with you?

OSCAR
(Fumbles with key)
Because I can't stand living alone, that's why.
(Puts key in door)
For crying out loud, I'm proposing to you. What do you want, a ring?

He opens door and they go in.

INT. OSCAR'S APARTMENT

They enter.

FELIX

Oscar, if you really mean it, there's a lot I can do around here. I'm very handy around the house. I can fix things. Do you know I fixed my wife's hair dryer?

OSCAR

I don't have a hair dryer. Blanche took it.

They're standing in the middle of the living room. Oscar goes to card table, picks up a beer can and sips it.

FELIX

I want to do something, Oscar. Let me do something.

OSCAR

All right, you can take my wife's initials off the towels, anything you want. . . . Come on, you can sleep in Brucey's bedroom.

Oscar crosses living room to Brucey's bedroom, followed by Felix.

FELIX

I can cook. You know I'm a terrific cook.

INT. BRUCEY'S BEDROOM—NIGHT—LIGHT CHANGE

It remains virtually untouched since the day Brucey left. Two small twin beds, bunnies painted on the headboards, a gingerbread house lamp on the table between the beds, toys all over, children's books on the shelves, finger paintings on the wall, one marked "Mommy" another marked "Dabby."

OSCAR
(Turns on light)
You don't have to cook. I got enough potato chips for a year.

FELIX
(Follows him into room)
Two meals a day at home, we'll save a fortune. We've got to pay alimony, you know.

OSCAR
(Pulling spread hastily off bed)
All right, Felix, you can cook.
(Playfully, he throws a pillow at Felix)

FELIX
Do you like leg of lamb?
(Puts pillow neatly back on bed)

OSCAR
Yes, I like leg of lamb.

FELIX
I'll make it this weekend.
(He starts to fold bedspread neatly)
I'll have to call Frances. She has my big pot.

OSCAR
(Shouts)
Will you forget Frances! We'll get our own pots. Don't drive me crazy before you move in.

The telephone rings in the living room.

FELIX
(Still folding spread)
Listen, Oscar, if I do anything that irritates you or gets on your nerves, don't be afraid to tell me.

Oscar has gone into living room to answer phone.

FELIX
It's your apartment, I don't want to irritate you or get on your nerves.

OSCAR'S VOICE
Hello? . . . Oh, hello, Frances.

Felix jumps at the sound of Frances's name.

INT. LIVING ROOM—NIGHT

Felix rushes into living room, waving his arms frantically for Oscar to see but lowering his panicky voice.

FELIX
I'm not here! I'm not here! You didn't see me! You don't know where I am!
I didn't call! I'm not here! I'm not here!

OSCAR
(Into phone)
Yes, he's here!

Felix throws up his arms. He paces nervously.

FELIX
How does she sound? Is she worried? What is she saying? Is she crying?
Does she want to speak to me? I don't want to speak to her.

OSCAR
(Into phone)
No, he's gonna stay here with me.

FELIX
And you can tell her I'm not coming back. I've had it there. I've taken just as
much as she has. I'm human too, you know. She's not the only one who
suffered in this marriage. Tell her. Tell her.

OSCAR
(Into phone)
Yes, he's fine.

FELIX

Don't tell her I'm fine! You heard me carrying on before. I was going to kill myself. What are you telling her I'm fine for?

OSCAR

(Into phone)
Yes, I understand, Frances.

FELIX

Does she want to speak to me? Ask her if she wants to speak to me.

OSCAR

Do you want to speak to him?

FELIX

(Sits)
Give me the phone. I'll speak to her.

OSCAR

Oh, you don't want to speak to him.

FELIX

She doesn't want to speak to me?

OSCAR

Yeah, I see. Right. Well, good-bye.
(He hangs up)

FELIX

She didn't want to speak to me?

OSCAR

No.

FELIX

Why did she call?

OSCAR

She wants to know when you're coming over for your clothes. She wants to have the room repainted . . . Listen, Felix, it's almost one o'clock. Let's go to sleep.
(Oscar gets up)

FELIX

Didn't want to speak to me, huh?

OSCAR

(Yawns, scratches)

I'll get you a pair of pajamas. You like stripes, dots or animals?

(He goes to bedroom)

FELIX

I want to kill myself and she's picking out colors.

OSCAR'S VOICE

I got slippers too. You like big bunny slippers?

FELIX

(Get's up, moves toward bedroom)

You know, I'm glad. Because she finally made me realize, it's over. It didn't sink in until just this minute.

OSCAR

(Returns with pajamas)

Felix, I want you to go to bed.

FELIX

My marriage is *really* over. Somehow it doesn't seem so bad now. I mean I think I can live with this thing.

OSCAR

Live with it tomorrow. Go to bed tonight.

FELIX

In a little while. I've got to think. I've got to start rearranging my life. Do you have a pencil and paper?

OSCAR

Felix, it's my house, I make up the bedtime.

(He throws pajamas at him)

FELIX

Oscar, please, I have to be alone for a few minutes. Go on, you go to sleep, I'll clean up.
(He starts cleaning up)
You can't leave dirt like this all night.

OSCAR

It's been here three weeks, it'll keep fresh until the morning.

FELIX

I couldn't sleep if I knew the room was like this.
(Cleaning up)
Go to bed, Oscar, I'll see you in the morning. I'll make breakfast.

OSCAR

You're not gonna do anything big, are you? Like rolling up rugs?

FELIX

(Still cleaning)
Ten minutes, that's all I'll be. I'll do the dishes and go right to bed.

Oscar gives up. He starts for his bedroom, taking off shirt.

OSCAR

He's gonna do the dishes.

Felix crosses to sofa and straightens out cushions.

FELIX

(Yells)
Oscar!

Oscar rushes out of bedroom, worried. Felix looks at him.

FELIX (CONT'D)

I'm going to be all right. It's going to take me a couple of days, but I'm going to be all right.

OSCAR
(Smiles)
Good! Well, good night, Felix.

He turns to go to bedroom as Felix begins to plump up pillow from the couch.

TWO SHOT—FELIX AND OSCAR

FELIX
(Plumping pillows)
Good night, Frances!

He continues puffing the pillows unaware of what he's said but Oscar stops dead in his tracks and turns and looks ominously at Felix.

DISSOLVE:

EXT. OSCAR'S APARTMENT HOUSE—FRONT ENTRANCE—NINE A.M.

People in the street are on their way to work. Felix and Oscar emerge from the building. Felix seems brighter this morning.

FELIX
(Smiles)
Well, I'll see you tonight, Os.

OSCAR
Right, Fel.

Felix smiles warmly at Oscar and gives him a playful punch in the shoulder.

FELIX
(Looks off)
Hey, there's my bus.

LONG SHOT

Felix runs off after the downtown bus as Oscar walks off in opposite direction. We show Felix just catching the bus and getting on.

FULL SHOT—OSCAR

As he walks down street, suddenly he hears Felix shout his name, "Oscar . . ." Oscar turns and looks.

FULL SHOT—BUS

It is driving down Riverside Drive and Felix has his head out the window.

FELIX
What should I make for dinner?

CLOSE-UP—OSCAR

Who grimaces.

EXT. SHEA STADIUM—DAY

The flags are up and the parking lot is full. The Mets are playing today.

INT. PRESS BOX—SHEA STADIUM—DAY

The game is in action down on the field. Oscar, puffing on his cigar, is behind his typewriter. Another sportswriter sits beside him. Oscar is typing. He takes a bite of a frankfurter and puts it down.

WRITER
(Defeated)
Well, that's the ball game.

OSCAR
It's not over yet.

WRITER
Ninth inning? Bases loaded? Hank Aaron is up and you expect the Mets to
hold on to a one-run lead?

OSCAR
Whatsa matter, you never heard of a triple play?

The other writer laughs derisively. A telephone rings.

CLOSE-UP—MAN IN PRESS BOX ONE ROW BEHIND OSCAR

He answers phone, then leans down.

MAN
Hey, Madison. Telephone.

CLOSE-UP—OSCAR

Intently watching game.

OSCAR
I'll call back.

CLOSE-UP—MAN

MAN
He says it's an emergency. He's got to speak to you.

CLOSE-UP—OSCAR

*He can't afford to miss this crucial moment in the game, but of course he must ac-
cept an emergency phone call. He gets up and turns around and answers the phone.
His back to the game.*

OSCAR
(Into phone)
Yeah?

CLOSE-UP—FELIX IN A STREET TELEPHONE BOOTH

Felix is holding a large paper bag filled with groceries.

FELIX
Oscar? I just want to call to make sure you don't eat any frankfurters at the game today because I'm making franks and beans for dinner.

Suddenly we hear an enormous roar.

CLOSE-UP—OSCAR AT THE GAME

The roar is from the twenty-one thousand people at the game, who are all on their feet. Oscar whirls around.

OSCAR
What happened?

CLOSE-UP—WRITER

He is on his feet, bursting with excitement.

WRITER
A triple play! The Mets did it! It was the greatest fielding play I ever saw in my life. You missed it, Oscar, you missed it.

CLOSE SHOT OF OSCAR

Steam is about to come out of both ears.

OSCAR
(Into phone)
Are you crazy? *Are you out of your mind?*

CLOSE-UP—FELIX IN PHONE BOOTH

FELIX
(On phone)
What's the matter? Don't you like franks and
beans? ... Hello? ... Oscar? ... Hello?

DISSOLVE TO:

EXT. RIVERSIDE DRIVE—OSCAR'S APARTMENT—NIGHT

*We hear a police siren and follow a police car as it speeds up Riverside Drive and pulls
up in front of Oscar's building. The door of the car opens and Murray the cop, in his
civvies, gets out, waves to the cops who drive away and enters the building quickly.*

INT. HALL—OSCAR'S FLOOR

*Murray hurries to the door and rings the bell. It opens and a disgruntled Oscar, in his
khaki slacks, baseball cap and cigar answers the door.*

MURRAY
I'm sorry I'm late, Oscar.

OSCAR
(Stops Murray with his hand)
Wipe your feet.

MURRAY
(Puzzled)
What?

OSCAR
If you know what's good for you, wipe your feet.

Murray, deeply puzzled, wipes his feet on the mat and then walks into the apartment.

INT. OSCAR'S APA\RTMENT—NIGHT

The game is in progress only the room bears little resemblance to the first poker scene we saw. The room sparkles, it shines with a dozen coats of Johnson's furniture polish. It is spotlessly clean. Not an ash is in an ashtray. Vinnie, Roy and Speed sit glumly around the table. Oscar returns to his seat. Murray takes off his Police Athletic League coat as he looks around the room in awe.

MURRAY

How's the game goin'? . . . Hey, what happened to the apartment?

OSCAR

It's been given the *Good Housekeeping* Seal of Approval. Deal him in.

Murray sits. Felix comes out of the kitchen pushing a tea cart with a neat tray of drinks and food and five linen napkins. He hums gaily as he pushes the cart down near the card table.

FELIX
(Smiles)
Hello, Murray.

Murray nods wordlessly. Felix takes the napkins one at a time, flicks them out to full length and places one on the lap of each player. Then he returns to the cart and very carefully, as a scientist would handle test tubes, he pours beer from can to glass, filling each one perfectly to the top.

FELIX

A cold glass of beer for Roy.
He begins to hand glass to Roy.

TWO SHOT—ROY AND FELIX

ROY
Thank you.

FELIX
(Stops)
Where's your coaster?

ROY
My what?

FELIX
Your coaster? The little round thing that goes under the glass.

ROY
(Looks on table)
I think I bet it.

CLOSE-UP—OSCAR

He throws in coaster, which was in his pile of chips.

OSCAR
Here. I knew I was winning too much.

CLOSE-UP—FELIX

FELIX
Always try to use your coasters, fellas.
(He has crossed back to the cart and picked up another drink)
Scotch and a little bit of water?

CLOSE-UP—SPEED

SPEED
Scotch and a little bit of water.
(He holds up coaster and says mockingly)
And I *have* my coaster.

FULL SHOT OF GAME

FELIX
(Nods approvingly at Speed)
I hate to be a pest but you know what wet glasses do.

Felix goes back to the cart where he picks up an ashtray and wipes it clean before setting it down on the table.

OSCAR
(Delicately)
They leave little rings on the table.

FELIX
(Puts ash tray down)
They leave little rings on the table.

OSCAR
(More delicately)
And we don't like little rings on our little tables.

FELIX
And we have a nice warm sandwich for Vinnie.

Like a headwaiter, Felix brings the sandwich on a dish to Vinnie, but first he wipes the table clean underneath with his napkin and even gives the underpart of the dish a wipe before setting it down.

CLOSE-UP—VINNIE

He whiffs and looks pleased.

VINNIE
Gee, it smells good. What is it?

TWO SHOT—FELIX STANDING NEXT TO VINNIE

FELIX
(Proudly)
Bacon, lettuce and tomato with mayonnaise on pumpernickel toast.

VINNIE
You mean you just made it?

FELIX
(*Smiles*)
One two three.

VINNIE
You put in toast and cooked bacon? Just for me?

CLOSE-UP—OSCAR

OSCAR
If you don't like it, he'll make you a meat loaf. Takes him five minutes.

FULL SHOT OF GAME

FELIX
You know me. I love to cook.

Felix is about to go, stops and cautions Vinnie. He tilts Vinnie's head forward.

FELIX
Try to eat over the dish. I just vacuumed the rug.
(*He crosses to tray*)
Oscar, what did you ask me for?

OSCAR
Two three-and-a-half-minute eggs and some petit fours.

FELIX
(*Smiles at the little joke, then remembers*)
A double gin and tonic. I'll be right back.

We follow Felix toward kitchen when he stops at an odd-looking machine on table against wall. He checks it.

FELIX (CONT'D)
Who turned off the de-humidifier?

MURRAY
The what?

FELIX
The de-humidifier!
(*He turns it back on*)
Don't play with this, fellas. I'm trying to get some of the grime out of the air.

Felix flicks at the "grimy" air with his napkin, shakes his head disapprovingly and goes into the kitchen. There is a moment of silence.

OSCAR
Murray, I'll give you two hundred dollars for your gun.

SPEED
(*Throws cards down*)
I can't take it anymore. I've had it up to here. In the last three hours we've played four minutes of poker. I'm not giving up my Friday nights to watch cooking and cleaning.

CLOSE-UP—ROY

His head is bent over the de-humidifier as he struggles to breathe.

ROY
I can't breathe. That lousy machine is sucking everything out of the air.

FULL SHOT OF TABLE

VINNIE
(*Chewing*)
Gee, this is delicious. Who wants a bite?

MURRAY
I didn't have supper. Is the toast warm?

VINNIE
Perfect. And not too much mayonnaise. It's really a well-made sandwich.

MURRAY
Cut me off a little piece.

VINNIE
Give me your napkin. I don't want to drop any crumbs.

Speed, who has been watching this in horror as Vinnie breaks off a piece of sandwich and gives it to Murray, slams his napkin down on table.

SPEED
(To Oscar)
Are you listening to this? Martha and Gertrude at the Automat?

CLOSE-UP—ROY

His head hangs lower and he rubs neck.

ROY
I'm telling you that thing could kill us. They'll find us here in the morning
with our tongues on the floor.

FULL SHOT OF GAME

SPEED
(Rising)
Do something, Oscar.
(Points to kitchen)
Get him back in the game.

OSCAR
Don't bother me with your petty little problems. You get this one stinkin' night
a week. I'm cooped up here with Mary Poppins twenty-four hours a day.

INT. KITCHEN

*Felix is very happy in his kitchen. He hums gaily as he puts ice tray back in refrig-
erator. The inside of the refrigerator is as neat and orderly as the rest of the house. We
hear Oscar's VOICE scream from inside, "Felix, get in here."*

FELIX
(Calls out)
I'm coming!

Felix is about to close the refrigerator when something catches his eye. He reaches in and takes out a half-smoked cigar. He holds it disgustedly and shakes his head.

FELIX
Slob! Slob! Slob!

INT. LIVING ROOM

Roy is banging on the de-humidifier with his fist.

ROY
It was better before. With the garbage and the smoke, it was better before.

TWO SHOT OF VINNIE AND MURRAY

VINNIE
(They're both eating)
Did you notice what he does with the bread?

MURRAY
What?

VINNIE
He cuts off the crusts. That's why the sandwich is so light.

MURRAY
And then he only uses the soft, green part of the lettuce. It's really delicious.

CLOSE-UP—SPEED

He looks to heaven.

SPEED
I'm going out of my mind.

FULL SHOT OF ROOM

OSCAR
(*Rising—walking toward kitchen door*)
I'm not gonna ask you again, Felix.

SPEED
(*Takes kitty box from off the record player and puts it on table and cashes in*)
Forget it, I'm goin' home. The day his marriage busted up was the end of our
poker game.

OSCAR
(*To Speed*)
You can't leave now. I'm a big loser.

SPEED
(*Putting on his coat*)
You got no one to blame but yourself.
(*He crosses to door*)
It's your fault. You're the one who stopped him from killing himself.

He exits angrily. Oscar stares after him.

OSCAR
He's right. The man is absolutely right.

THREE SHOT—VINNIE, MURRAY AND OSCAR

MURRAY
(*To Vinnie*)
Are you gonna eat that pickle?

Oscar has come around and stands between the two of them watching.

VINNIE
I wasn't thinking of it. Why? Do you want it?

MURRAY

Unless you want it? It's your pickle.

VINNIE

No, no. Take it. I don't usually eat pickle.

Vinnie holds the paper plate with the pickle out to Murray. Oscar slaps the plate from underneath, sending the pickle flying through the air. Oscar is furious!

OSCAR

Deal the cards.

MURRAY

What did you do that for?

OSCAR

Just deal the cards. You want to play poker, deal the cards. You want to eat, go to a delicatessen.
(To Vinnie)
Keep your sandwich and your pickles to yourself. I'm losing fifty-three dollars and everybody's gettin' fat!
(He screams)
Felix!

MED. SHOT—KITCHEN DOOR

Felix comes out.

FELIX
What?

CLOSE-UP—OSCAR

OSCAR
Close the stinkin' restaurant and sit down! We got a poker game in here.

FELIX
(Innocently)
Oh, is it up to me?

FULL SHOT—GROUP

Felix starts for table then spies something in horror on the floor. He picks it up, looks around in anger.

FELIX
Who threw a pickle on my floor? I don't think that's funny.

He takes it off to the kitchen.

ROY
(Sniffs around)
What is that smell? . . . Disinfectant!
(He smells cards)
It's the cards! *He washed the cards!*

Roy is angrily putting on his coat as Oscar paces like a caged lion.

ROY
I'm getting out of here. I can't stand any more.

OSCAR
(Turns)
Where are you going?

ROY
I've been sitting breathing cleaning fluid and ammonia for three hours.
Nature didn't intend for poker to be played like that.

He exits and slams the door.

MED. SHOT—FELIX COMING OUT OF KITCHEN

FELIX

Okay, I'm ready to play.

OSCAR

(Dejected)

Good. We got just enough for handball.

Felix crosses to table.

FELIX

Where is everybody?

OSCAR

You got the nerve to ask that? I just got sterilized out of fifty-three dollars.

FELIX

(To others)

Gee, I'm sorry, fellows. Is it my fault?

VINNIE

(At window)

No. I guess no one feels like playing tonight. Well, I'd better be going too.
Gotta get up early.
(Walking to poker table)
Bebe and I are driving to Asbury Park for the weekend.

FELIX

(He smiles warmly)

Just the two of you, heh? Gee, that's nice. You always do things like that
together, don't you?

VINNIE

(Counting money, a big winner)

We have to. I don't know how to drive.
(He starts out)
You coming, Murray?

Murray is up and putting on his jacket.

MURRAY

Yeah, why not? I gotta stop off and get Mimi a hero sandwich and a frozen
eclair. . . .
(On way to door, shrugs)
Marriage! Boy, those two playboys sure got the life, eh, Vinnie?

VINNIE

Yeah. Some life those playboys got.

Vinnie and Murray exit laughing good-naturedly.

TWO SHOT—FELIX AND OSCAR SITTING AT TABLE

FELIX

(Staring after them)
That's funny, isn't it, Oscar? They think we're happy. They really think
we're enjoying ourselves.
(He begins to straighten up)
They don't know, Oscar. They don't know what it's like living alone, do
they?

*Felix gives a short, ironic laugh, tucks the napkin under his arm and starts to pick up
the dishes from the table.*

OSCAR

(Stares emptily ahead)
I'd be immensely grateful to you, Felix, if you didn't clean up just now.

FELIX

(Puts dishes on tray)
It's only a few things.
(He stops and looks back at door)
Playboys! Us! That's really funny. You know I think they actually envy us.
They should only know.

Felix clears some more stuff from the table. We STAY on Oscar, sitting there morosely.

OSCAR

Felix, leave everything alone. I'm not through dirtying up for the night.

He takes some poker chips from the table and tosses them messily on the floor.

Felix starts spraying the air in the room with a deodorizer spray.

FELIX
(Spraying)
But don't you see the irony of it, Oscar? Don't you see it?

OSCAR
(Waves the mist from in front of his face)
Yes, I see it.

FELIX
(Puts can down)
No, you don't. I really don't think you do.

OSCAR
(Controlling himself)
Felix, I'm telling you I see the irony of it.

FELIX
(Pauses, sits down, looks at Oscar)
Then tell me. What is it? What's the irony?

Oscar looks directly into Felix's face. He says the next deliberately and menacingly, but without raising his voice.

OSCAR

The irony is . . . unless we can come to some other arrangement . . . I'm
gonna kill you.
(He rises and walks toward the hallway)
. . . That's the irony.

Felix looks after him, worried.

FELIX
What's wrong, Oscar?

OSCAR
(Stops)
There's something wrong with this system, that's what's wrong. I don't think that two single men living alone in a big eight-room apartment should have a cleaner house than my mother.

FELIX
What are you talking about? I'm not asking you to do it. You don't have to clean up.

OSCAR
What you do is worse. You're always in my bathroom hanging up my towels. Whenever I smoke you follow me around with an ashtray. Last night I found you washing the kitchen floor, shaking your head and moaning, "Footprints, Footprints."

FELIX
I didn't say they were yours.

OSCAR
Well, they *were* mine, damn it. I have feet and they make prints. What do you want me to do, climb across the cabinets?

He gets up.

FELIX
No, I want you to walk on the floor.

OSCAR
I appreciate that. I really do.

Felix is straightening out the pictures on the hallway wall.

FELIX

I'm just trying to keep the place livable. I didn't realize I irritated you that much.

OSCAR

Leave the pictures alone.

FELIX

I'm just trying to even them up.

OSCAR

I *want* them uneven. They're my pictures. Even your own pictures.

FELIX

(He seems hurt, he returns to the living room)
I was wondering how long it would take.

OSCAR

How long what would take?

FELIX

Before I got on your nerves.

OSCAR

(Looks at Felix)
I didn't say you get on my nerves. . . . Please, don't do that.

FELIX

Well, it's the same thing. You said I irritated you.

OSCAR

You said you irritated me. I didn't say it.

FELIX

Then what *did* you say?

OSCAR

I don't remember *what* I said. What's the difference what I said?

FELIX

It doesn't make any difference. I was just repeating what I thought you said.

OSCAR
(Losing patience)
Well, don't repeat what you *thought* I said. Repeat what I *said*. My God, that's irritating.

FELIX
You see. You *did* say it!

OSCAR
I don't believe this whole conversation.

Felix picks up a teacup from the table and paws it.

FELIX
Oscar, I'm—I'm sorry. I don't know what's wrong with me.

TWO SHOT—OSCAR PACING BEHIND FELIX

OSCAR
And don't pout. If you want to fight, we'll fight. But don't pout. Fighting I win, pouting you win.

FELIX
You're right. Everything you say about me is absolutely right.

OSCAR
(Angrier)
And don't give in so easily. I'm *not* always right. Sometimes *you're* right.

FELIX
You're right. I do that. I always figure I'm in the wrong.

OSCAR
Only this time you *are* wrong and I'm right.

FELIX
Oh, leave me alone.

OSCAR
And don't sulk. That's the same as pouting.

CLOSE-UP—FELIX

FELIX
I know. I know.
(*He squeezes cup with anger*)
Damn me, why can't I do one lousy thing right?

He suddenly stands up and cocks his arm back about to hurl the cup angrily against the wall or door. Then he thinks better of it, puts the cup down carefully and sits.

CLOSE-UP—OSCAR

OSCAR
Why didn't you throw it?

CLOSE-UP—FELIX

FELIX
I almost did. I get so insane with myself sometimes.

TWO SHOT—TOGETHER

Oscar has moved closer to Felix.

OSCAR
Then why don't you throw the cup?

FELIX
Because I'm trying to control myself.

OSCAR
Why?

FELIX

What do you mean, why?

OSCAR

Why do you have to control yourself? You're angry, you felt like throwing a cup, why don't you throw it?

FELIX

Because there's no point to it. I'd still be angry and I'd have a broken cup.

CLOSE-UP—OSCAR

OSCAR

How do you know how you'd feel? Maybe you'd feel wonderful. Why do you have to control every single thought in your head? Why don't you let loose once in your life? Do something that you *feel* like doing, and not what you *think* you're supposed to do. . . . Stop controlling yourself, Felix. Relax! Get drunk! Get angry! C'mon, *break the lousy cup!*

CLOSE-UP—FELIX

Oscar has worked him up to a pitch. He defiantly hurls the cup against the wall, smashing it. Then he grabs his shoulder in pain.

FELIX

Owww! I hurt my arm.

He contorts in pain and rubs arm. He sits near the fireplace.

FULL SHOT—LIVING ROOM

OSCAR

You're hopeless! You're a hopeless mental case.

FELIX

I'm not supposed to throw with that arm. I have bursitis.

OSCAR

Why don't you live in a closet? I'll leave your meals outside the door and slide in the papers.

FELIX

All right, cut it out, Oscar. That's the way I am. I get hurt easily. I can't help it.

OSCAR

You're not going to cry, are you? I think all those tears dripping on the arm is what gave you bursitis.

FELIX

I may not be the easiest one in the world to live with, but you could have done a lot worse for yourself . . .
(He crosses into kitchen)
A lot worse.

INT. KITCHEN

Felix at the sink is putting on rubber gloves ready to soak the dishes.

OSCAR

How?

FELIX

I put order into this house. For the first time in months you're saving money, sleeping on clean sheets, eating *hot* meals for a change. *I* did that.

OSCAR

That's right. And then at night after we've had your halibut steak, I spend the evening watching you Saran Wrap the leftovers . . .
(He takes a hard-boiled egg out of the refrigerator)
. . . Felix, when are you and I gonna have a little fun? Some relaxation?

FELIX

What are you talking about? We have fun. . . . Eat over the sink!

Felix pushes Oscar to sink as he continues to straighten up in the kitchen.

OSCAR
(Eating egg over sink)
You don't understand. Getting a clear picture on channel two isn't my idea of whoopee!

FELIX
We don't always watch TV. Sometimes we read, we talk. . . .

OSCAR
(Wipes hands on pants)
No, no. I read and *you* talk. I try to work and *you* talk. I go to sleep and *you* talk. We got your life arranged pretty good but I'm still looking for a little entertainment.

FELIX
What are you saying? That I talk too much?

OSCAR
No, I'm not complaining. You've got a lot to say. What's worrying me is that I'm beginning to listen.

FELIX
You won't hear another peep out of me.

He takes scissors out of side cabinet drawer.

OSCAR
You're not gonna give me a haircut, are you?

FELIX
I'm going to cut up some greens. I thought I'd make some coleslaw for tomorrow.

OSCAR
(Grabs scissors out of his hand)
I don't want coleslaw tomorrow! I want to have some fun tonight!

FELIX
I thought you liked my coleslaw.

OSCAR

I *love* your coleslaw. I'll take your coleslaw to work with me. But not tonight!
Please, Felix. Let's get out of the house.

FELIX

(Moving out)

All right. Let's go. I only made it because of you. I don't even like coleslaw.

OSCAR

(Ecstatic)

We're getting out! We're finally getting out.

FELIX

(As they're exiting)

What is it, too sweet? I don't have to use sugar. If you don't like sugar in your
coleslaw, say so. . . .

DISSOLVE:

INT. BOWLING ALLEY—CLOSE-UP—A BOWLING BALL—NIGHT

The ball lowers and we see Felix's eyes peering over the rim, aiming his shot.

FULL SHOT—INT. BOWLING ALLEY

Felix is on the line, aware of his sore shoulder. He winds up and lets the ball go.

CUT TO BALL

We follow it down the lane until it hits the remaining three pins.

CLOSE-UP—FELIX

He turns and smiles, rubbing his shoulder.

CLOSE-UP—FELIX

He stands at table next to Oscar just behind shooting line, marking his score.

FELIX
(Looks at Oscar)
When you're right, you're right. A person has to get out of the house once in a while.

We hear the high-pitched giggle of girls.

MED. SHOT—NEXT LANE

Four high school–aged girls are in the next booth. A very attractive girl stands on the line, the others offering encouragement.

TWO SHOT—OSCAR AND FELIX

OSCAR
(Gets up to bowl)
Yeah, well, bowling is all right for exercise, Felix, but it's not the kind of relaxation I had in mind.
(He looks over to next lane)

MED. SHOT—NEXT LANE

The girl bowls the ball, looking very tantalizing.

TWO SHOT—FELIX AND OSCAR

Oscar is still looking at other lane, Felix is writing on scorepad.

OSCAR
The night was made for other things.

FELIX
(Writing)
Like what?

OSCAR
(Still looking)
Like unless I get to touch something soft in the next two weeks, I'm in big trouble.

Felix looks up at Oscar, walking around him.

FELIX
You mean women?

OSCAR
(Still looking off)
If you want to give it a name, all right, women.

FELIX
That's funny. You know I haven't thought about women in weeks.

OSCAR
I fail to see the humor.

FELIX
Listen, when Frances and I were happy together, I used to look plenty. I mean I'm as normal as any guy. But since we broke up, I don't even know what another woman looks like.

OSCAR
(Leans closer)
I could point one out to you . . . or I could make a phone call.

FELIX
What are you saying?

OSCAR
(Leans over closer)
I'm saying let's spend one night talking to someone with higher voices than us.

FELIX
You mean? . . .

OSCAR
That's what I mean.

FELIX
Oh. Well, I can't.

OSCAR
Why not?

FELIX
Well, it's all right for you. But I'm still married.

OSCAR
(Trying to push Felix out of the way)
You can *cheat* until the divorce comes through.

FELIX
(Turns away from Oscar)
I'm just not ready yet, Oscar. I really don't want to discuss it. Let's bowl, heh.

Oscar aims ball, lowers it, starts in motion.

CUT TO BALL

We follow it down the lane until it hits the pins, a perfect strike.

INT. POOL HALL—BILLIARD BALLS ON POOL TABLE—NIGHT

Another ball slams into the pack, breaking the formation and sending them all over the table. PULL BACK, FULL SHOT OF POOL TABLE. Oscar has just shot and Felix stands watching with cue stick. We are in a pool hall somewhere in the West Eighties.

FELIX
Listen, I intend to go out. I get lonely too. But I'm just separated a few weeks. Give me a little time.

OSCAR
(Planning his next shot)
There isn't any time left. I saw *TV Guide* and there's nothing on this
week . . . 12 in the corner. . . . What am I asking you? All I want to do is have
dinner and some laughs with a couple of girls.

He shoots and sinks shot.

FELIX
Why do you need me? Can't you go out yourself?

OSCAR
(Chalks cue and plans next shot)
Because I may want to come back to the apartment. And if we walk in and
find you washing the windows, it puts a damper on things.
(He shoots and misses)

FELIX
I'll take a pill and go to sleep.

Felix lines up a shot.

OSCAR
Why take a pill when you can take a girl?

FELIX
Because I'd feel guilty, that's why. Maybe it doesn't make any sense to you but
that's the way I feel.

Oscar hits the ball toward the pocket. Felix grabs the ball before it falls in.

FELIX
Go ahead and shoot.

CLOSE-UP—OSCAR

He reacts in his usual manner.

INT. TAVERN IN WEST EIGHTIES—PINBALL MACHINE—NIGHT

The ball bounces down the board, banging coils, lighting up. PULL BACK and we see Felix at the helm, Oscar watching. Oscar is sipping a beer.

FELIX

. . . Anyway, who would I call? The only single girl I know is my secretary and I don't think she likes me.

Oscar look at Felix. For the first time he has gotten through to Felix. Oscar beams at the prospect.

OSCAR
(Excited, looks at Felix)

Leave that to me. There's two sisters who live in our building. English girls. One's a widow, the other's a divorcee. They're a barrel of laughs.

FELIX

How do you know?

OSCAR

I was trapped in the elevator with them last week. I can call them now. Please, Felix, for my sake, say yes.

CLOSE-UP—FELIX

FELIX
(Deliberates)

Well . . . if it means that much to you . . .

TWO SHOT—OSCAR AND FELIX

Oscar jumps up happily, grabs Felix by the shoulders and shakes him.

OSCAR

That's the Felix I've been waiting for.
(He fishes in pocket for coins)
This'll be perfect.

FELIX
What do they look like?

OSCAR
(Has coins in his hand and he searches for a dime)
Don't worry. Yours is very pretty.

Oscar turns and walks out of frame. We stay on Felix, who looks worried.

DISSOLVE:

MEDIUM SHOT—PHONE BOOTH

Oscar is inside, door closed. Felix outside, pacing apprehensively. We see Oscar laughing exaggeratedly into phone. He hangs up and opens the door, exiting the booth.

OSCAR
Seven-thirty tomorrow. We're all set.

FELIX
Wait a minute. Which one do I get?

OSCAR
The divorcee.

FELIX
Why do I get the divorcee?

OSCAR
I don't care. You want the widow?

FELIX
No, I don't want the widow. I don't even want the divorcee. I'm just doing this for you.

OSCAR

Look, take whoever you want. When they come in the door, just point to the
sister of your choice . . . I just want to have some laughs.
(Finishing his beer)
Come on! Let's get a good night's sleep.

FELIX
(Muttering)
What are they? Old—young?—About thirty . . . thirty-five . . . older? Where
did you meet them? Did they want to meet me?

INT. BATHROOM—OSCAR'S APARTMENT—NIGHT

We see the figure of Oscar, back to us, standing at the sink, brushing his teeth.

OSCAR
(Calling out to Felix)
Now don't forget and suddenly call one of them Frances. It's Gwendolyn and
Cecily.

INT. BRUCEY'S BATHROOM

FELIX
(At sink brushing his teeth)
No. Frances. Gwendolyn and Cecily.

INT. OSCAR'S BEDROOM

Oscar, in his underwear, is singing happily, getting into bed. He Watusis into bed.

INT. FELIX'S BEDROOM

Felix, not very happy, in fact gloomy, mumbles to himself as he gets into bed.

FELIX

I can imagine what kind of girls *he* knows. . . . What if my kids see me? . . . Hmp . . . I'm going to nightclubs with foreign girls and I got two American kids to support.

Felix turns to wall as if to sleep.

INT. OSCAR'S BEDROOM

Oscar is in bed. Suddenly the lights flick on.

CUT TO:

DOOR

Felix stands there.

FELIX

Where are we going to have dinner?

CLOSE-UP—OSCAR

OSCAR

(He looks up)

Anywhere you say. Chinese? Italian?

CLOSE-UP—FELIX

FELIX

You mean a restaurant? The four of us? It'll cost a fortune.

CLOSE-UP—OSCAR IN BED

OSCAR

We'll cut down on laundry. We won't wear socks on Thursdays.

CLOSE-UP—FELIX

FELIX

We can't afford restaurants. We'll have dinner here. I'll cook, we'll save
thirty, forty dollars.

CLOSE-UP—OSCAR

He sits up. Looks worried.

OSCAR

What kind of double date is that? You'll be in the kitchen all night?

CLOSE-UP—FELIX

FELIX

No, I won't. I'll put it up in the afternoon. Once I get my potatoes in, I'll have
all the time in the world.
*(He snaps fingers as he remembers something. He goes to phone next to Oscar's bed
and starts to dial. Oscar looks at him worriedly)*

TWO SHOT—FELIX DIALING—OSCAR IN BED

OSCAR

What happened to the whole new Felix? Who are you calling?

FELIX

Frances. I want to get her recipe for meat loaf. The girls'll be crazy about it.

*Felix waits for his call to come through as Oscar sinks into bed and pulls the pillow
over his head.*

DISSOLVE:

INT. TELEVISION NEWS ROOM—DAY

CUT TO WALL FEATURING FIVE OR SIX CLOCKS THAT DE-
NOTE THE TIME ALL OVER THE WORLD. IN NEW YORK IT
IS TEN TO FIVE.

*PAN DOWN and we are in a busy office of a television news department. Felix is
working feverishly at a typewriter. He glances at his watch, panics, grabs his coat,
puts it on as he rips the papers out of typewriter and deposits them in a box on another desk.*

EXT. BROADWAY—WEST EIGHTIES—SUPERMARKET—DAY

Felix enters hurriedly.

MONTAGE

*Felix at various counters, stalls, departments, scurrying around quickly throwing
items into his cart. Squeezing melons . . . etc.*

MEAT DEPARTMENT

*Butcher is weighing chopped ground on scale, Felix is directing butcher to add a lit-
tle more, no that's too much, take off a little more. The butcher fumes at Felix.*

EXT. RIVERSIDE DRIVE—OSCAR'S APARTMENT HOUSE— EVENING

*Oscar, carrying his jacket and a package containing one laundered shirt in one hand,
and a bottle of wine in a brown paper bag in the other, with a straw hat cocked back
on his head, skips gaily down the street humming and into his building.*

DOOR OF OSCAR'S APARTMENT FROM INSIDE

*The door opens and Oscar steps in whistling and then stops and gapes, wide-eyed at
what he sees.*

INT. APARTMENT

PAN around room. It is a joy to behold. Curtains have been ironed and hung, flowers fill various jars, and the sight of sights is the dining table. It is set beautifully for four, a lace tablecloth covers the table, and two tall tapered candles sit in the center.

MED. SHOT—OSCAR

He walks into the room, surveying everything, ecstatic. He puts bottle on table.

OSCAR
(Calls out, playfully)
I'm home, dear!

Oscar goes toward the bedroom. Felix pushes the kitchen door open and watches Oscar go into the bedroom. Felix goes back into the kitchen. Oscar now comes out of bedroom putting on fresh shirt.

OSCAR
(Coming down hallway)
Beautiful, just beautiful. Something *wonderful* is going on in that
kitchen. . . . No, sir, there's no doubt about it. I'm the luckiest man on earth.

CLOSE-UP—FELIX

He is seated in the chair, playing with ladle, steaming silently. Oscar stands behind him.

CLOSE-UP—OSCAR

OSCAR
I got the wine.
(Takes wine out of bag)
Batard Montrachet, six and a quarter. You don't mind do you, pussycat?
We'll walk to work this week.

CLOSE-UP—FELIX

fumes silently.

MED SHOT—OSCAR

He is fixing tie, which was around his neck when he came out.

> **OSCAR**
> Hey, no kidding, Felix, you did a great job. One little suggestion? Let's come down a little with the lights . . .

He turns one lamp off.

> **OSCAR**
> . . . and up very softly with the music.

He crosses to record player and inspects some records.

> **OSCAR (CONT'D)**
> . . . You think Debussy goes good with meat loaf? . . . What's the matter Felix?

CLOSE-UP—FELIX

sitting silently fuming.

MED. SHOT—OSCAR

> **OSCAR**
> *(Puts records back)*
> Something's wrong, I can tell by your conversation.

MED. SHOT—FELIX

He plays with ladle. We hear Oscar's voice.

OSCAR'S VOICE
All right, Felix. What is it?

FELIX
(Looking straight ahead)
What is it? Let's start with what time do you think it is?

CLOSE-UP—OSCAR

OSCAR
What time? I don't know, seven-thirty?

CLOSE-UP—FELIX

FELIX
Seven-thirty? Try eight o'clock.

CLOSE-UP—OSCAR

OSCAR
All right, so it's eight o'clock. So?
(He fixes tie)

CLOSE-UP—FELIX

FELIX
So you said you'd be home at seven.

TWO SHOT

Felix sitting, Oscar standing behind him tucking shirt into trousers.

OSCAR
Is that what I said?

FELIX

That's what you said. "I will be home at seven" is what you said.

OSCAR

Okay, I said I'd be home at seven and it's eight. So what's the problem?

CLOSE SHOT—FELIX

FELIX

If you knew you were going to be late, why didn't you call me?

TWO SHOT—SAME AS BEFORE

OSCAR
(*Buttoning shirt sleeves*)
I couldn't call you, I was busy.

FELIX

Too busy to pick up a phone?

OSCAR

I was in the office, working.

FELIX

Working? Ha!

OSCAR

Yes. Working.

FELIX

I called your office at seven o'clock, you were gone.

OSCAR
(*Combs his hair*)
It took me an hour to get home. I couldn't get a cab.

FELIX

Since when do they have cabs in Hannigan's bar?

OSCAR
(He stops and looks at Felix)
Wait a minute. I want to get this down on a tape recorder because no one'll believe me. You mean now I have to call you if I'm coming home late for dinner?

FELIX
(Rising, walking to kitchen, slamming door behind him)
Not *any* dinner. Just the ones I've been slaving over since five o'clock this afternoon to help save *you* money to pay your wife's alimony.

OSCAR
(Controlling himself)
Felix, this is no time to have a domestic quarrel. We have two girls coming down any minute.

FELIX
(Coming out of kitchen)
You mean you *told* them to be here at eight o'clock?

OSCAR
(He crosses to couch)
I don't remember what I said. Seven-thirty, eight o'clock. What difference does it make.
(He tries to take a cracker and some dip from the cocktail table in front of him)

MED. SHOT—FELIX

He crosses to sofa.

FELIX
I'll tell you what difference. You told me they were coming at seven-thirty. You were going to be here at seven to help me with the hors d'oeuvres. At seven-thirty they arrive and we have cocktails. At eight o'clock we have dinner. It is now eight o'clock.
(Walking back to kitchen)
My meat loaf is finished. If we don't eat in fifteen seconds, the whole damned thing'll be *dried out!*

CLOSE-UP—OSCAR

looks up.

> **OSCAR**
> Oh, God, help me.

CLOSE-UP—FELIX

> **FELIX**
> *(At kitchen door)*
> Never mind helping *you.* Tell him to save the meat loaf.

Felix goes into kitchen.

INT. KITCHEN

> **OSCAR**
> *(Entering)*
> Can't you keep it warm?

> **FELIX**
> What do you think I am, the Magic Chef? I'm lucky I got it to come out at eight o'clock. What am I going to do?

> **OSCAR**
> I don't know. Keep pouring gravy on it.

> **FELIX**
> What gravy?

> **OSCAR**
> Don't you have any gravy?

> **FELIX**
> *(Storms over to Oscar. He is working himself up to a lather)*
> Where the hell am I going to get gravy at eight o'clock?

MED. SHOT—OSCAR

OSCAR
I thought it comes when you cook the meat.

MED. SHOT—FELIX

He looks at Oscar incredulously.

FELIX
When you *cook* the meat? You don't know the first thing you're talking about. You have to *make* gravy, it doesn't *come!*

MED. TWO SHOT—FELIX—OSCAR

OSCAR
You asked my advice, I'm giving it to you.

FELIX
Advice?
(He shakes ladle in Oscar's face)
You didn't know where the kitchen was till I came here and showed you.

OSCAR
You wanna talk to me, put down that spoon.

FELIX
(Exploding with rage, again waves ladle in his face)
Spoon? You dumb ignoramus, it's a ladle. You don't even know it's a ladle.

OSCAR
All right, Felix, get ahold of yourself.

MED. SHOT—FELIX

FELIX
(At the kitchen door)
You think it's so easy? Go on. The kitchen's all yours. Go make a meat loaf for four people who come a half hour late.

Felix goes into living room.

INT. LIVING ROOM—OSCAR

He follows and says to no one in particular.

OSCAR
Listen to me. I'm arguing with him over gravy.
(The doorbell rings)

TWO SHOT—FELIX AND OSCAR

FELIX
(Jumps up)
Well, they're here. Our dinner guests. I'll get a saw and cut the meat.

Oscar stops him.

OSCAR
Stay where you are.

FELIX
I'm not taking the blame for this dinner.

OSCAR
Who's blaming you? Who even cares about the dinner?

FELIX
(Banging his own chest with ladle)
I care. I take pride in what I do. And you're going to explain to them exactly what happened.

OSCAR
All right, you can take a color picture of me coming in at eight o'clock. Now take off that stupid apron because I'm opening the door.

He rips the apron (which is really a towel tucked into his pants) off. Felix suddenly feels denuded. Oscar crosses to the door. STAY on Felix. He takes his suit jacket, which has been draped over dining chair.

FELIX

I just want to get one thing clear. This is the last time I ever cook for you. Because people like you don't even appreciate a decent meal. That's why they have TV dinners.

Felix puts on his suit jacket, still preoccupied with his angry thoughts. He is still holding the ladle and puts it through the sleeve of the jacket as if it were an extension of his hand. He buttons his jacket.

OSCAR AT DOOR

OSCAR

You through?

FELIX'S VOICE

I'm through.

OSCAR

Then smile.

Oscar opens the door. TWO GIRLS poke their heads in. They are in their early thirties and are somewhat attractive. They are in neat, prim summer dresses. Appetizing, but not flagrant. And they are definitely English.

OSCAR

. . . . Well, hello.

GWEN

Hallo.

CECILY

Hallo.

Oscar opens the door and they step in.

GWEN

I do hope we're not late.

OSCAR

No, no. You timed it perfectly. Come in, come in . . . Er, Felix, I'd like you to
meet two elevator acquaintances of mine—
(He points to them)
Gwendolyn and Cecily.

CECILY

(He made a mistake, she corrects him)
Cecily and Gwendolyn.

CLOSE-UP—FELIX

*He manages a weak smile. He is still fondling the ladle, then notices it and sticks it
in the chair.*

MED. SHOT—GIRLS AND OSCAR

OSCAR

That's right, Cecily and Gwendolyn . . . er . . . was it Robin? Cardinal?

GWEN

Wrong both times. It's Pigeon.

OSCAR

Pigeon. Right. The Pigeon Sisters.

GWEN

Or as our friends in Chelsea used to say, "The Coo-Coo Pigeon Sisters."
*(She says "Coo" like a pigeon cooing; she and Cecily laugh at their familiar joke as
does Oscar)*

OSCAR

I like that. The Koo-Koo Pigeon Sisters. Well, girls, I'd like you to meet my
roommate and our chef for the evening, Felix Ungar.

FULL SHOT—GIRLS, OSCAR AND FELIX BELOW THEM

CECILY
(Holds out hand)
Heh d'yew dew?

Felix goes up the two steps to the entrance landing and shakes Cecily's hand.

FELIX
How do you do?

GWEN
(Extends hand)
Heh d'yew dew?

FELIX
(Shakes her hand)
How do you do.

But Felix has stepped up too close and he finds himself standing nose to nose with Oscar. It is a tight little group and very awkward.

OSCAR
Well, we did that beautifully. Why don't we sit down and make ourselves comfortable?

Felix steps aside and ushers the girls down into the room. There is ad-libbing and a bit of confusion and milling about as they all squeeze between the armchair and the couch to get to the couch, simply because that's the way nervous Felix has led them.

CLOSE SHOT—FELIX

squeezing through with girls. As he does, Felix inhales and sniffs with nose as he suddenly reacts to the girls' perfume. It's his old allergy again. He grabs his nose and makes a strange noise with his throat. The girls sit on sofa.

FULL SHOT OF FOUR

Felix is moving far away from girls as Oscar motions to Felix to stop acting like a nut.

FELIX
(Whispers)
Perfume! It's the perfume!

He makes a few low-volume moose bellows to clear his ears again. Oscar, annoyed, sits in the armchair next to the girls and Felix sits farther away from the girls on the love seat. Finally, they have all settled.

THREE SHOT—CECILY, GWEN AND OSCAR

CECILY
This is ever so nice, isn't it, Gwen?

GWEN
(Looks around)
Lovely. And much nicer than our flat. Do you have help?

OSCAR
Er, yes. I have a man who comes in every night.

CECILY
Aren't you the lucky one.

Cecily, Gwen and Oscar all laugh at her joke. Oscar turns and looks at Felix while still laughing.

CLOSE-UP—FELIX

There is no response. He either doesn't get it or is too nervous to hear human conversation.

MED. SHOT—OSCAR, GWEN AND CECILY

OSCAR
(Rubs hands)
Well, isn't this nice. . . . I was telling Felix yesterday about how we happened
to meet.

GWEN
Oh? Who's Felix?

OSCAR
(A little embarrassed, points to Felix)
He is!

GWEN
(Acknowledging Felix)
Oh, yes, of course. I'm sorry.

CLOSE-UP—FELIX

He nods very slightly accepting her acknowledgment.

MED. SHOT—OSCAR, CECILY AND GWEN

CECILY
You know it happened to us again this morning.

OSCAR
What did?

GWEN
We were stuck in the elevator.

OSCAR
Really? Just the two of you?

CECILY
And poor old Mr. Kessler from the third floor. We were in there half an
hour.

OSCAR
No kidding? What happened?

GWEN
Nothing much, I'm afraid.

Cecily and Gwen both laugh at their latest joke, joined by Oscar. Once again he looks over at Felix.

CLOSE-UP—FELIX

Again no response.

MED. SHOT—THREESOME AGAIN

OSCAR
Well, this really is nice.

CECILY
And ever so much cooler than our place.

GWEN
It's like equatorial Africa on our side of the building.

CECILY
Last night was so bad Gwen and I sat there in nature's own cooling ourselves in front of the open fridge. Can you imagine such a thing?

OSCAR
Er, I'm working on it.
(*Oscar laughs*)

CLOSE-UP—FELIX

He is about to yawn, but he stifles it.

BACK TO THREESOME

GWEN
Actually it's impossible to get a night's sleep. Cec and I really don't know what to do.

OSCAR
Why don't you sleep with an air conditioner?

GWEN
We haven't got one.

OSCAR
I know. But we have.

The group laughs again.

GWEN
Oh, you! I told you about that one, didn't I, Cec?

CLOSE-UP—FELIX

FELIX
They say it may rain Friday.

GROUP

They all stare at Felix. Oscar gives Felix a wink and finger sign as if to say, "Well done."

GWEN
Oh?

CECILY
That should cool things off a bit.

OSCAR
I wouldn't be surprised.

CLOSE-UP—FELIX

FELIX
(He sees one line isn't enough for conversation. He needs two)
Although sometimes it gets hotter after it rains.

MED. SHOT—FULL GROUP OF FOUR

GWEN
Yes, it does, doesn't it?

Felix jumps up, mostly wanting to get out of there, picks up the ladle and heads toward kitchen.

FELIX
Dinner's served.

Oscar jumps up and stops him.

OSCAR
No, it isn't.

FELIX
Yes, it is.

OSCAR
No, it isn't. I'm sure the girls would like a cocktail first.
(He elbows Felix)
Wouldn't you, girls?

GWEN
Well, I wouldn't put up a struggle.

OSCAR
There you are.
(To Cecily)
What would you like?

CECILY
Oh, I really don't know. What have you got?

FELIX

Meat loaf.

OSCAR

(Glares)

She means to drink.

(To Cecily)

We have everything. And what we don't have, I mix in the medicine cabinet.

(He crouches next to her)

What'll it be?

TWO SHOT—CECILY AND GWEN

CECILY

Oh, a double vodka.

GWEN

Cecily, not before dinner.

CECILY

My sister. She watches over me like a mother hen. . . . Make it a *small* double vodka.

FULL SHOT OF GROUP

OSCAR

A small double vodka.

(To Gwen)

And for the beautiful mother hen?

GWEN

Oh, I'd like something cool. I think I would like a double Drambuie with some crushed ice, unless you don't have the crushed ice.

OSCAR

I was up all night with a sledgehammer. I shall return.

(He rises)

Oscar goes toward the kitchen. Felix chases after him.

TWO SHOT—FELIX AND OSCAR

FELIX
(Whispers)
Where are you going?

OSCAR
(Now at kitchen door)
To get the refreshments.

FELIX
(Starting to panic)
Inside? What'll I do?

OSCAR
You can finish the weather report.

He exits into the kitchen. Felix calls after him:

FELIX
Don't forget to look at my meat.

He turns and faces the girls. He braces himself for the coming ordeal. He crosses to the chair Oscar sat in and crosses his legs nonchalantly, but he is very ill at ease. He fidgets with his tie as girls look at each other awkwardly. It is silent. Felix realizes he can no longer get away with the tie fidgeting and smiling, so he plunges in.

FELIX
Er, Oscar tells me you're sisters.

CECILY
Yes, that's right.
(She looks at Gwen)

FELIX
From England.

GWEN
Yes, that's right.
(She looks at Cecily)

FELIX
I see.
(Silence, then his little joke)
We're not brothers.

CECILY
Yes, we know.

FELIX
Although I am *a* brother. I have a brother who's a doctor. He lives in Buffalo. That's upstate in New York.

GWEN
(Takes a cigarette from her purse)
Yes, we know.

FELIX
You know my brother?

GWEN.
No. We know that Buffalo is upstate in New York.

FELIX
Oh.

He gets up, takes a cigarette lighter from the side table and moves to light Gwen's cigarette.

CECILY
We've been there. Have you?

FELIX
No. Is it nice?

CECILY
Lovely.

Felix closes the lighter on Gwen's cigarette and turns to go back to his chair, taking the cigarette, now caught in the lighter, with him. He notices the cigarette and hastily gives it back to Gwen, stopping to light it once again. He puts the lighter back on the table and sits down, brushing some dirt off the table, which he just spotted. There is a pause.

FELIX

Isn't that interesting? . . . How long have you been in the United States of America?

CECILY

Almost four years now.

FELIX

(Nods)

Uh huh . . . Just visiting?

GWEN

No. We live here.

FELIX

And you work here too, do you?

GWEN

Yes, we're secretaries for a health club.

CECILY

People bring us their flabby bodies and we pound them into shape.

(She illustrates with hands)

GWEN

Actually, if you're interested, we can get you ten percent off.

CECILY

Off the price, not off your body.

FELIX

Yes, I see.

He laughs nervously. They all laugh. Suddenly he shouts toward kitchen, as if for help.

FELIX
Oscar! Where's the drinks?

INT. KITCHEN

Oscar is at the refrigerator pulling ferociously at the ice tray, which won't budge.

OSCAR
(Shouts)
Coming! Coming!
(He lips obscenities at ice tray)

THREESOME IN LIVING ROOM

CECILY
What field of endeavor are you engaged in?

FELIX
I write the news for television.

CECILY
Oh, fascinating.

GWEN
Where do you get your ideas from?

FELIX
(He looks at her as though she were a Martian)
From the news.

GWEN
Oh, yes, of course. Silly me.

CECILY
Maybe you can mention Gwen and me in one of your news reports.

FELIX

Well, if you do something spectacular, maybe I will.

CECILY

Oh, we've done spectacular things but I don't think we'd want it spread all
over the telly, do you, Gwen?
(They both laugh)

FELIX

(Laughs too, then cries out for help again)
Oscar!

INT. KITCHEN

Oscar has his shoe off and is banging at the stuck ice tray with the heel.

OSCAR

(Shouts)
I'm coming! I'm coming!

THREESOME IN LIVING ROOM

FELIX

It's such a large apartment, sometimes you have to shout.

GWEN

Just you two baches live here?

FELIX

Baches? Oh, bachelors. We're not bachelors. We're divorced. That is, Oscar's
divorced. I'm *getting* divorced.

CECILY

Oh. Small world. We've cut the dinghy loose too, as they say.

GWEN

Well, you couldn't have a better matched foursome, could you?

FELIX

No, I suppose not.

GWEN

Although technically I'm a widow. I was divorcing my husband, but he died before the final papers came through.

FELIX

Oh, I'm awfully sorry.
(Sighs)
It's a terrible thing, isn't it? Divorce.

GWEN

It can be. If you haven't got the right solicitor.

CECILY

That's true. Sometimes they can drag it out for months. I was lucky. Snip, cut and I was free.

GWEN

But of course, that's all water under the bridge now, eh? Er, I'm terribly sorry, but I think I've forgotten your name.

FELIX

Felix.

CECILY

Like the cat.

Felix takes his wallet out of pocket.

GWEN

Well, the Pigeons will have to beware of the cat, won't they?
(Laughs)

CECILY

(Nibbles on nuts from dish)
Mmm, cashews, lovely.

FELIX
(Takes snapshot from wallet)
This is the worst part of breaking up.
(Hands picture to Cecily)

BACK TO GROUP

CECILY
Childhood sweethearts, were you?

FELIX
No, no. That's my little boy and girl.

Cecily gives picture to Gwen who puts on a pair of glasses from her purse.

FELIX
He's seven, she's five.

CECILY
(Looks again)
Oh, sweet!

FELIX
They live with their mother.

GWEN
I imagine you must miss them terribly.

CLOSE-UP—FELIX

who reflects ruefully.

FELIX
I can't stand being away from them. But, that's what happens with divorce.

THREE SHOT—FELIX, GWEN AND CECILY

Felix takes back the picture and looks at it longingly.

CECILY

When do you get to see them?

FELIX

Every night. I stop there on my way home. Then I take them on the weekends, and I get them on holidays and July and August.

CECILY

Oh! Well, when is it that you miss them?

FELIX

Whenever I'm not there. If they didn't have to go to school so early, I'd go over and make them breakfast. They love my French toast.

GWEN

You're certainly a devoted father.

FELIX

It's Frances who's the wonderful one.

CECILY

She's the little girl?

FELIX

No, she's the mother. My wife.

GWEN

The one you're divorcing?

FELIX

(Nods)

Mm. She's done a terrific job bringing them up. They always look so nice, they're so polite. Speak beautifully. Never, "Yeah." Always, "Yes." They're such good kids. And she did it all. She's the kind of woman who—ah, what am I saying? You don't want to hear any of this.

(Puts picture back in wallet)

CECILY

Nonsense. You have a right to be proud. You have two beautiful children and a wonderful ex-wife.

INT. KITCHEN

Oscar is standing over the sink with a hammer, banging away at ice tray in sink.

GROUP IN LIVING ROOM

Felix takes out another picture from wallet and shows it to girls.

FELIX

That's Frances. My wife.

GWEN

(Looks at picture)

Oh, she's pretty. Isn't she pretty, Cecy?

CECILY

Oh, yes. Pretty. A pretty girl. Very pretty.

FELIX

(Takes it and looks at it)

Yes, she's pretty.

(Shows them another snap)

Isn't this nice?

(Gwen takes picture)

BACK TO GROUP

GWEN

There's no one in the picture.

FELIX

I know. It's a picture of our living room. We had a beautiful apartment.

GWEN

Oh, yes. Pretty. Very pretty.

CECILY

(Glancing over at picture)

Those are lovely lamps.

FELIX

Thank you.

(Takes picture back)

We bought those lamps in Mexico on our honeymoon.

(Looks at it again)

I used to love to come home at night. That was my whole life. My wife, my kids, my apartmen—

(He suddenly breaks down and sobs)

TWO SHOT—CECILY AND GWEN

They look at each other, it's an awkward moment.

CECILY

Does she have the lamps now too?

FELIX

(Nods, trying to control sobbing)

I gave her everything. The children, the lamps, ev—

(Turns his head away)

I'm sorry.

(Takes out a handkerchief and covers his eyes)

Please forgive me. I didn't mean to get emotional.

THREE SHOT

FELIX

. . . Would you like some potato chips?

He reaches over and hands bowl to girls, but doesn't look at girls.

GWEN

You mustn't be ashamed. I think it's a rare quality in a man to be able to cry.

CECILY

So do I. I think it's sweet. Terribly, terribly sweet.

FELIX

Please, you're just making it worse.

GWEN
(Getting emotional)
It's so refreshing to hear a man speak so highly of the woman he's divorcing.
Oh, dear.
(She takes out her handkerchief)
Now you've got me thinking about poor Sydney.

CECILY

Oh, Gwen, please don't.

GWEN

It was a good marriage at first. Everyone said so. Didn't they, Cecy? Not like you and George.

The unhappy past suddenly returns to Cecily. Her eyes fill with tears.

CECILY

That's right. George and I were never happy. Not for one single solitary day.

She remembers her grief, grabs her hanky and dabs her eyes. All three are now sitting with hankies at their eyes. They are all crying.

FELIX

Isn't this ridiculous?

GWEN

I don't know what brought this on. I was feeling so good a few minutes ago.

CECILY
(Bawling)
I haven't cried since I was fourteen.

GWEN
Oh, dear. Oh, dear. Oh, dear!

KITCHEN DOOR

Oscar bursts happily into the room with a tray full of drinks. He is all smiles.

OSCAR
(Like a corny M.C.)
Is ev-ry-buddy happy?

He suddenly stops when he looks at the group.

OSCAR
What the hell happened?

FULL SHOT—ALL FOUR

Felix and the girls quickly try to pull themselves together.

FELIX
Nothing, nothing.

OSCAR
What do you mean, nothing? I'm gone three minutes and I walk into a funeral parlor. What did you say to them?

Felix gets up and walks to the window, wiping his eyes.

FELIX
I didn't say anything. Don't start in again, Oscar.

CLOSE-UP—OSCAR

OSCAR

I can't leave you alone for five seconds. Well, if you really want to cry, go
inside and look at your meat loaf!

CLOSE-UP—FELIX

FELIX

Oh, my gosh.
(He rushes to kitchen)
Why didn't you call me? I told you to call me.
(He goes into kitchen)

OSCAR AND GIRLS

OSCAR

I shoulda warned you about Felix, girls. He's a walking soap opera.

GWEN

I think he's the dearest thing I ever met.

CECILY

He's so sensitive. So fragile. I just want to bundle him up in my arms and
take care of him.

MEDIUM SHOT—OSCAR

*He has been holding Gwen's drink. He is so shocked by their attitude toward Felix,
he puts Gwen's drink back on tray, picks up his and takes a healthy swig.*

OSCAR

Well, when he comes out of that kitchen, I think you may have to.

KITCHEN DOOR

Felix sticks his head out. He is an unhappy man. Smoke comes out the door.

FELIX

I'll get some corned beef sandwiches. I'll be right back.

He goes back into kitchen, coughing.

TWO SHOT—GIRLS

They are full of sympathy as they jump up and head for kitchen.

CECILY

Wait, Felix, maybe we can fix it.

INT. KITCHEN

The room is filled with smoke. Felix is opening kitchen window and holding the charred ruins of meat loaf in the pan out the window. The girls come in, followed by Oscar. They all cough.

OSCAR

Let me see it!

FELIX

(Holds charred pan for him to see)
See what? Six dollars worth of ashes? I'd throw it down the incinerator except it won't burn *twice.*

He throws it on stove, turns and pouts out window.

TWO SHOT—GIRLS

They are sympathetic to Felix's plight and want to make it a successful evening for him.

CECILY

I've got a wonderful idea. Why don't we have dinner in our place? If you don't mind potluck?

CLOSE-UP—OSCAR

sees the fantastic possibilities.

OSCAR
(Big grin)
I'm crazy about potluck.

GROUP SHOT

GWEN
Of course it's awfully hot up there. You'll have to take off your jackets.

OSCAR
It's getting even better. We can always open up the refrigerator.
(He laughs)

CECILY
Give us five minutes to get into our cooking things.

Cecily and Gwen walk into living room. Oscar follows. Felix is still pouting at kitchen window.

OSCAR
Can't you make it four?

GWEN
Don't forget the wine.

OSCAR
How could I forget the wine?

CECILY
And a corkscrew.

OSCAR
And a corkscrew.

GWEN

And Felix.

OSCAR

No, I won't forget Felix.

CECILY

Ta, ta.

OSCAR

Ta, ta.

GWEN

Ta, ta.

The girls exit.

OSCAR

(Throws a kiss at the closed door)

You bet your tea and crumpets, "Ta, Ta!"

Oscar grabs Felix happily and wheels him around.

OSCAR

(Continuing)

Felix, I love you.

He kisses Felix on forehead.

OSCAR

You've just overcooked us into one hell of a night. Come on get the ice
bucket, I'll get the wine.

He skips gaily out of kitchen.

INT. LIVING ROOM

Oscar comes out kitchen door. He goes to dining table and picks up wine. Felix comes out of kitchen, morose.

FELIX
. . . I'm not going.

He crosses toward his bedroom. Oscar looks up.

OSCAR
What?

FELIX
(Crossing room)
I said I'm not going.
(He goes into his room and closes door)

Oscar cannot quite believe what he's heard. He picks up records in his other arm, then goes to Felix's room and opens door.

INT. FELIX'S ROOM

Felix lies down on bed. He reaches over to shelf next to bed and selects a book to read. It is Bambi. *Oscar comes into room, holding records and wine.*

OSCAR
Are you out of your mind? Do you know what's waiting for us up there?
You've just been invited to spend the evening in a two-bedroom hothouse
with the Kookoo Pigeon Sisters. What do you mean you're not going?

FELIX
(Glancing at book)
I have nothing more to say to them. I already told them about my brother in
Buffalo. I've used up my conversation.

OSCAR

Felix, they're crazy about you. They told me. One of them wants to wrap you up and make a bundle out of you. You're doing better than I am. Get the ice bucket.

CLOSE-UP—FELIX

FELIX

Don't you understand? I cried. I cried in front of two women.

CLOSE-UP—OSCAR

OSCAR

And they loved it. I'm thinking of getting *hysterical.* . . . Come on, get the bucket.

CLOSE-UP—FELIX

FELIX

Don't you see? Emotionally I'm still tied to Frances and the kids. I don't want to discuss it anymore.
(He starts for kitchen)
I'm gonna scrub the pots and wash my hair.
(He goes into kitchen)

OSCAR
(In doorway of kitchen)
Your greasy pots and your greasy hair can wait. You're coming upstairs with me.

INT. KITCHEN

Felix is at sink, rolling up his sleeves.

FELIX
I'm not going.

OSCAR
(Entering kitchen)
What am I going to do with two girls? Felix, if I miss this opportunity, I'll never forgive you.

Felix wordlessly pours hot water into burnt pot and begins to scrub with brush.

OSCAR
. . . You mean you're not going to make any effort to change. This is the person you're going to be . . . until the day you die?

FELIX
(Still scrubbing)
We are . . . what we are!

Oscar glares at him, then turns and goes into living room.

INT. LIVING ROOM

Oscar storms out to the steps of the front entrance, pauses, walks to the nearest window and opens it furiously. He shouts in to Felix:

OSCAR
It's *twelve* floors, not eleven!

He storms out the door and slams it hard.

DISSOLVE:

THE NEXT DAY—EXT. OSCAR'S APARTMENT HOUSE— RIVERSIDE DRIVE—DAY

It is late afternoon. We hear the distant rumble of thunder.

SHOT OF DARK, RAIN CLOUDS

We see a burst of lightning and hear a loud thunderclap.

EXT. STREET

The rain suddenly descends in torrents.

INT. LOBBY OF OSCAR'S BUILDING—DAY

Oscar runs in drenched. He looks at his cigar, which has been doused by the rain.
Felix suddenly rushes in from outside, equally drenched. He takes out his hand-kerchief to wipe his drenched neck when he sees Oscar. They look at each other, then look away. Wordlessly, they cross to elevator. Oscar presses button and the door opens. He goes in elevator. Without acknowledging his existence, Felix goes in after him.

INT. ELEVATOR—OSCAR'S APARTMENT HOUSE—DAY

Oscar presses the "12" button. Felix, wanting to be independent, presses "12" after him. Oscar glares at him. The doors close and the elevator goes up. They both take out soaking wet newspapers and read them in hostile silence. The door opens and they go out.

INT. HALL—OSCAR'S FLOOR—DAY

They both go down hall, each taking out his key. Oscar puts his key in door and opens it. He steps in apartment, slamming the door in Felix's face. Felix burns, then opens door with his own key and goes in.

INT. LIVING ROOM—OSCAR'S APARTMENT

Oscar tosses wet newspaper on table with a thud. Oscar takes off his dripping hat and shakes it vigorously on the rug. Felix enters holding his shoes.

INSERT—RUG ON FLOOR

We see huge, wet, dark footprints on the rug as Oscar walks off.

CLOSE-UP—FELIX

who shakes head as if to say "If he's asking for it, he's going to get it." He begins to pick up the wet things that Oscar has discarded.

DISSOLVE:

INT. OSCAR'S APARTMENT—DAY

The door of Oscar's bedroom opens and Oscar comes out buttoning a dry shirt. He has a fresh cigar.

We hear the whir of a vacuum cleaner. We follow Oscar into the living room, and there is Felix, also in fresh, dry clothes, vacuuming the rug. Oscar looks at the plug in the wall and pulls it out. The machine stops. Felix turns and looks at Oscar.

Oscar takes cellophane wrapper off cigar, crumples it and throws it on floor directly in front of Felix. Felix glares at him. Then Oscar steps up on the sofa in a determined effort to squash the puffed-up pillows. He gets off and with one foot, squashes the pillow on the armchair. Then he crosses over to wall and tilts a picture so that it now hangs crooked. Then he settles down on the sofa with his newspaper.

Felix has been watching all this. He picks up cellophane wrapper, crosses to table where Oscar's hat is and picks up a wrapper. Then Felix takes the vacuum cleaner and takes it off into kitchen.

The cord of the vacuum is still extended into the living room.

INT. KITCHEN—DAY

Felix attempts to put the vacuum into the closet and then realizes the cord is still extended into the living room. He starts to pull it in.

INT. LIVING ROOM—DAY

Oscar sees the cord is being pulled into room, quickly gets up and steps on the cord, preventing it from being pulled in. We see it being yanked a few times.

INT. KITCHEN—DAY

Felix is yanking on cord. Then his arm raises, about to give it a strong yank.

INT. LIVING ROOM—DAY

Oscar still has his foot on the cord, then suddenly lifts it off the cord as it is violently yanked. The cord flies toward kitchen and we hear an enormous crash of a body into pots and pans. Oscar chuckles and goes back to sofa. He has won Round One.

RAIN CLOUDS OUTSIDE

The clouds darken, the lightning strikes and the thunder roars as the storm without and within worsens.

INT. KITCHEN

Felix is over stove cooking spaghetti. He rubs his back in pain from the fall he just took. He strains the spaghetti. Rain pounds against the window.

INT. LIVING ROOM

Oscar is sprawled out on the sofa watching a movie on television. He is enjoying the program.
    Felix comes out of kitchen with his dinner, a plate of spaghetti. He crosses from the dining table to the television set and turns it off. The set whines out.

CLOSE-UP—FELIX—DINING ROOM

who smells his spaghetti, sits and mixes dinner with fork and spoon.

FULL SHOT—LIVING ROOM

Oscar gets up, crosses to the dining room, picks up spray deodorizer and sprays all around the dining table, and for a final gesture, sprays right into Felix's spaghetti. Felix tosses the fork into the dish as Oscar goes to a sofa and picks up a book.

FELIX
All right, how long is this going to go on?

OSCAR
Are you talking to me?

FELIX
That's right, I'm talking to you.

OSCAR
What do you want to know?

FELIX
I want to know if you're going to spend the rest of your life not talking to me. Because if you are, I'm going to buy a radio.

OSCAR
You had your chance to talk last night.
(Takes key out of pocket)
There's a key to the back door. If you stick to the hallway and your room, you won't get hurt.
(He slams key down on table)

FELIX
Meaning what?

OSCAR
Meaning that if you want to live here, I don't want to see you, I don't want to hear you and I don't want to smell your cooking. Now get this spaghetti off my poker table.

FELIX
Ha, ha, ha.

OSCAR
What the hell's so funny?

FELIX
It's not spaghetti, it's linguini.

Oscar picks up the plate of linguini, crosses to the doorway of kitchen and hurls it up and into the kitchen.

OSCAR
(Turns)
Now it's garbage!

FELIX
You're crazy! I'm a neurotic nut but you're crazy!

OSCAR
I'm crazy, heh? That's really funny coming from a fruitcake like you.

FELIX
(Goes to kitchen door, opens it halfway and looks in)
I'm not cleaning that up.

OSCAR
Is that a promise?

FELIX
Did you hear what I said? I'm not cleaning it up. It's your mess.
(He looks in again)
Look at it. Hanging all over the walls.

OSCAR
(Crosses to door where Felix is and looks)
I like it!

He closes door and walks away. Felix follows Oscar down hallway.

FELIX
You'd just let it lie there, wouldn't you? Until it turns hard and brown and . . . yich, it's disgusting, I'm cleaning it up.

He goes into the kitchen.

OSCAR
(Yells)
Leave it alone!
(He rushes toward kitchen)
You touch one strand of that linguini and I'll punch you right in the sinuses.

Oscar runs into the kitchen. We hear scuffling. Pots crash.

MED. SHOT—OTHER DOOR OF APARTMENT

Felix rushes out into hallway, being chased by Oscar. Felix closes the iron gates just before Oscar reaches him.

FELIX
Oscar, why don't you take a tranquilizer?

OSCAR
(Opening iron gates)
Go to your room. Do you hear me? Go to your room.

Felix walks to Brucey's bedroom through kitchen.

OSCAR
(Walking down hallway)
I'm warning you, if you want to live through this night, you'd better tie me up and lock your doors and windows.

He walks to his bedroom. The door to Brucey's bedroom opens a crack, revealing Felix's nose, one eye and his mouth.

FELIX
(Calmly)
All right, Oscar, I'd like to know what's happened.

We hear Oscar's voice roar.

OSCAR'S VOICE
WHAT'S HAPPENED??

Frightened, Felix quickly closes the door. . . . Then it opens a crack again.

FELIX
That's right. Something must have caused you to go off the deep end like this.
(He opens door more)
What is it? Something I said? Something I did?

OSCAR
Don't start me.

CLOSE-UP—FELIX

Felix opens the door all the way and walks to Oscar's bedroom—entering.

FELIX
What is it? The cooking? The cleaning? The crying?

CLOSE-UP—OSCAR—INT. BEDROOM

OSCAR
(In bed)
I'll tell you exactly what it is.
It's the cooking, cleaning and the crying. It's the talking in your sleep. It's the moose calls that open your ears at two o'clock in the morning.
(Oscar bellows in imitation)

MED. SHOT—FELIX

who looks hurt and crosses into room.

MED. SHOT—OSCAR

OSCAR

I can't take it anymore, Felix. I'm cracking up. Everything you do irritates
me. And when you're not here, the things I know you're gonna do when you
come in irritate me. Like right now you're gonna pout and say, "I see."

CLOSE-UP—FELIX

He walks around the room. He pouts.

FELIX

I see.

CLOSE-UP—OSCAR

He nods, acknowledging his prediction.

OSCAR

Ahuh. . . . You leave me little notes on my pillow. I told you a hundred times,
I can't stand little notes on my pillow. "We're all out of corn flakes,
F.U.". . . . It took me three hours to figure out that F.U. was Felix Ungar.

THE WINDOW

The thunder roars as the rain continues.

FULL SHOT—INT. OSCAR'S BEDROOM

OSCAR

It's not your fault, Felix. It's a rotten combination.

*Felix crosses to window and looks out. A little rain has come in through the crack of
the sill and he takes out handkerchief and wipes it.*

FELIX

I get the picture.

OSCAR

That's just the frame. The picture I haven't even painted yet. I've got a typewritten list in my office of the "Ten Most Aggravating Things You Do That Drive Me Berserk".... But last night was the topper. I had it all set up with that English Betty Boop and her sister and I wind up drinking tea all night and telling them *your* life story.

Felix crosses to Oscar.

FELIX

Don't blame me. I warned you not to make the date in the first place.

He makes his point by shaking his finger in Oscar's face.

OSCAR

Don't point that finger at me unless you intend to use it.

FELIX

All right, Oscar, get off my back. Get off! Off!

He moves threateningly close to Oscar, then realizing he may get hit, he warily steps back quickly.

OSCAR

What's this, a display of temper? I haven't seen you really angry since the day I dropped my cigar in your pancake batter.

FELIX

Oscar, you're asking to hear something I don't want to say. But if I say it, I think you'd better hear it.

INT. OSCAR'S BEDROOM

OSCAR
(Gets up facing Felix)
If you've got anything on your chest besides your chin, you'd better get it off.

Oscar stands on opposite side of bed.

FELIX
All right, I warned you.

They both lean in like two bucks about to engage in mortal combat.

FELIX
. . . . You're a wonderful guy, Oscar. You've done everything for me. If it weren't for you, I don't know what would have happened to me. You took me in here, gave me a place to live and something to live for. I'll never forget you for that.
(Moves nose-to-nose)
You're *tops* with me, Oscar.
(Felix walks away from Oscar)

OSCAR
(Relaxes)
If I've just been told off, I think I may have missed it.

FELIX
It's coming now. You're also one of the biggest slobs in the world.

OSCAR
I see.

FELIX
And completely unreliable.

OSCAR
Finished?

FELIX

Undependable.

OSCAR

Is that it?

FELIX

And irresponsible.

OSCAR

Keep going, I think you're hot.

FELIX

That's it. I'm finished. *Now* you've been told off. How do you like that?

He stands erect, hitches up his belt like a Western hero and strides to other side of room.

OSCAR

Good. Because now I'm gonna tell *you* off. For six months I lived alone in this apartment. All alone in eight rooms. I was dejected, despondent and disgusted. Then *you* moved in. My dearest and closest friend. And after three weeks of close, personal contact, I'm about to have a nervous breakdown!
(He really is)
Do me a favor. Move into the kitchen. Live with your pots, your pans, your ladle and your meat thermometer. When you want to come out, ring a bell and I'll run into the bedroom.
(Breaking down)
I'm asking you nicely, Felix . . . as a friend. . . . Stay out of my way.

Oscar is practically in tears as he heads for the bathroom. He goes in.

FELIX

(Tentatively)
Walk on the papers, will you, I just washed the floor in there.

THE BATHROOM DOOR

Oscar steps out. His eyes are bulging and he is breathing fire through his nose. He is a rampaging rhinoceros. He starts for Felix.

FELIX

All right, keep away from me. Keep away from me.

Felix darts out of the bedroom with Oscar in hot pursuit. Felix darts into another room and Oscar chases him in as Felix emerges from another door with Oscar racing after him.

OSCAR
(Chasing him)
I'm gonna kill you! This is the day I'm gonna kill you.

Felix runs out the front door, slamming it after him. Oscar opens it and goes running after him.

INT. HALLWAY

Felix runs into hall, Oscar is not pursuing. Suddenly Felix confronts Oscar coming out of the service entrance. Felix sees the elevator. It opens as a woman steps out with packages. Felix rushes in and presses button. Oscar tries to maneuver around the woman and her packages, and by the time he does, the elevator door has closed. It starts up. Oscar pounds on the entrance door and yells up.

FELIX

Hit me and you got yourself one sweet lawsuit, Oscar.

OSCAR

Come on, let me get in one shot. You pick it, head, stomach or kidneys.

Oscar runs past the bewildered woman and up the stairs.

EXT. ELEVATOR ON TOP FLOOR

Felix, frightened, runs out and looks around. He goes to staircase and looks down.

INT. STAIRCASE LANDING ONE FLOOR BELOW

Oscar is rushing up.

INT. TOP FLOOR

> **FELIX**
> *(Yells down)*
> Can I talk to you calmly?

INT. STAIRS—OSCAR RUNNING UP

> **OSCAR**
> First you'll bleed, then you'll talk.

INT. STAIRS TO ROOF

Felix runs up the last little flight of stairs, through the door that leads to the roof. Oscar is now right behind him and runs up the last flight and out the door.

EXT. ROOF OF BUILDING—DAY—RAIN

The rain is pouring down. Felix backs away as Oscar now stalks him slowly.

> **OSCAR**
> There's no place for you to go now, Felix . . . except down!

> **FELIX**
> Are you out of your mind? If you want to fight, come on down to the living room. I'm getting wet.

Felix backs away, putting a fan vent between them.

OSCAR

I don't want you in my living room. I don't want you in my bedroom, or in my bathroom, my kitchen, my hall, my elevator, my building . . . I DON'T WANT YOU AT ALL!

FELIX

What are you talking about?

OSCAR

It's all over, Felix. The whole marriage. We're getting an annulment. Don't you understand? I don't want to live with you anymore. I want you to pack your things, tie them up with your Saran Wrap and get out of here.

FELIX

You mean actually move out?

The rain continues to drench them as the thunder roars overhead.

OSCAR

Actually, physically and immediately.
(Points off roof)
There! You can move into the Museum of Natural History. I'm sure you'll be very happy dusting around the Egyptian mummies.

FELIX

You mean move out, right this minute.

OSCAR

If you can make it sooner, I'd appreciate it.

Felix relaxes and walks closer to Oscar, as though what he has to tell him is of monumental importance.

FELIX

You know . . . I've got a good mind to really leave.

CLOSE-UP—OSCAR

He looks to heaven for help.

OSCAR
Why doesn't he hear me? I know I'm talking, I recognize my voice.

TWO SHOT—FELIX AND OSCAR

FELIX
Because if you really want me to go, then I'll go.

OSCAR
Then go. I want you to go. So go.

FELIX
Boy, you're in a bigger hurry than Frances was.

OSCAR
Take as much time as she gave you. I want you to follow your usual routine.

FELIX
In other words, you're throwing me out.

OSCAR
Not in other words. Those are the perfect ones.

FULL SHOT—ROOF

FELIX
All right. I just wanted to get the record straight. Let it be on *your* conscience.

He pushes Oscar aside and heads for the door on roof. Oscar runs after him.

OSCAR
What? What? Let *what* be on my conscience?

Felix opens door but stands there, still in rain.

FELIX

I'm perfectly willing to stay and clear the air of our differences. But you refuse, right?

OSCAR

Right. I'm sick and tired of you clearing the air. That's why I want you to leave.

FELIX

Fine. But remember, what happens to me is your responsibility. Let it be on your head!

He goes into building and closes door. Oscar stands there in the rain, dumbfounded.

OSCAR
(Yells)
Wait a minute, dammit. Why can't you be thrown out like a decent human being?
(He opens door)

INT. STAIRS COMING DOWN FROM ROOF

Oscar runs after Felix.

OSCAR (CONT'D)
. . . . I've been looking forward to throwing you out all day and now you've even taken the pleasure out of that.

FELIX

Forgive me for spoiling your fun.

He walks down and out of FRAME.

DISSOLVE:

INT. OSCAR'S APARTMENT—LIVING ROOM

Felix comes out of his bedroom with suitcase. Oscar paces in living room.

FELIX

I'm leaving now, according to your wishes and desires. Either I'll pick up the rest of my clothes . . . or someone else will.
(*Meaning the executors of the late Felix Ungar's estate*)

Felix starts for door and opens it but Oscar runs past him and shuts the door, blocking exit with his body.

OSCAR

You're not leaving here till you take it back.

FELIX

Take what back?

OSCAR

"Let it be on your head." What the hell is that, *The Curse of the Cat People?*

FELIX

I can't leave if you're blocking the door.

Felix gently pushes Oscar aside, opens the door and goes out.

OSCAR

Is this how you left that night with Frances? No wonder she wanted to have the room painted—I'm going to have yours dipped in bronze.

FELIX

Get out of my way, please.

INT. HALL

Felix walks to elevator, as Oscar comes out of apartment after him. Felix waits for elevator. The elevator stops, the door opens and Felix walks in solemnly with his suitcase.

OSCAR

Felix . . . where will you go?

Felix has his finger on button.

FELIX
(*His famous, final speech*)
Oh come on, Oscar. You're not really interested, are you?

Felix gives Oscar a weak smile, presses button and door closes. The elevator goes down as Oscar stands there a moment, tortured. Then he bangs on door and yells down.

OSCAR
All right, Felix, you win. We'll try to iron it out. Anything you want. Come back, Felix . . . Felix? Felix? . . . *Don't leave me like this*—you louse!

Oscar pounds weakly on the door. He reminds us much of Kay Francis after John Boles has left for good in the final scene of Craig's Wife.

DISSOLVE TO:

INT. OSCAR'S LIVING ROOM—SHOT OF MEN'S FEET PACING—DAY—RAIN HAS STOPPED

We PULL BACK and we are in Oscar's living room. Roy and Murray are pacing nervously. Speed is at the window. Oscar and Vinnie are seated.

MURRAY
I'm telling you, I'm worried. I know Felix, he's gonna try something crazy.

VINNIE
You mean you just threw him out?

OSCAR
That's right. I threw him out. It was my decision. All right? I admit it. Let it be on my head.

VINNIE
Let what be on your head?

OSCAR
How should I know. Felix put it there. Ask him!

SPEED
And he's out there somewhere.

OSCAR
(Defensive—he stands)
Listen, he was driving us all crazy with his napkins and ashtrays and bacon, lettuce and tomato sandwiches. You all said so.

ROY
We didn't say kick him out.

OSCAR
(Walking behind sofa)
Who did I do it for? I did it for us.

ROY
Us?

OSCAR
Yes! Yes! Do you know what he was planning for next Friday night's poker game? As a change of pace? Do you have any idea?

VINNIE
What?

OSCAR
A luau! An Hawaiian luau! Spareribs, roast pork, fried rice. They don't play poker like that in Honolulu!

SPEED
He's out there alone.

MURRAY
Now I'm really worried.

OSCAR
Then why don't we stop worrying and start looking?
(He grabs his jacket)
Come on, what are you standing there?

ROY
How are we gonna find him? It's a big city.

OSCAR
(At door)
We'll look for a man with a suitcase who's crying.
(He rushes out)

DISSOLVE TO:

EXT. BROADWAY AND UPPER EIGHTIES—DUSK

We see a police car driving down Broadway.

INT. POLICE CAR—LIVE

Murray is driving. Oscar sits in front with him. In back are Speed, Vinnie and Roy. Murray is still in civvies.

MURRAY
They're not gonna like this at the station. You're not supposed to look for a missing person with a missing car.

OSCAR
Take it outta my taxes. We'll try his apartment first.

EXT. BROADWAY INTO 86TH STREET—DUSK

Police car turns corner.

EXT. APARTMENT HOUSE—334 WEST 86TH STREET—DUSK

The police car is double-parked in front of building. Vinnie comes out of building and gets into car.

INT. OF POLICE CAR

VINNIE
Frances hasn't heard from him since he called to get her recipe for meat loaf.

MURRAY
Where to now?

OSCAR
Cruise along Riverside Drive.

MURRAY
This is crazy, Oscar. Why don't we call the cops?

OSCAR
(*Glares at him*)
Drive the car!

EXT. 334 WEST 86TH STREET—DUSK

Police car pulls away.

EXT. POLICE CAR DRIVING ALONG RIVERSIDE DRIVE—DUSK

The police car stops at a red light. Another police car pulls up beside it, stopping also for the red light.

MED. SHOT—POLICEMEN IN OTHER CAR

They look in and see Murray and all the civilians in his car.

FIRST COP
What are you doing, Murray?

MURRAY
(Nervously)
Off-duty arrest. I caught them gambling.

The other cop nods as Murray pulls away.

DISSOLVE TO:

EXT. SHOT OF CENTRAL PARK WEST—DUSK

The police car cruises along the street.

INT. POLICE CAR

They all look out windows.

SPEED
We already combed the whole West Side. Why don't we go back to the
apartment and wait to hear something.

OSCAR
(Looking very morose)
Because I'm afraid we're liable to hear something.

MURRAY
The poor guy.

OSCAR
Will you stop saying "The poor guy." What about me? I got a lousy curse on
my head. . . .

VINNIE
Let's go back, Oscar. He'll show up.

OSCAR

I know him. He'll kill himself to spite me. His ghost will come back following me around the apartment . . . haunting and cleaning . . . haunting and cleaning.

The others look at Oscar sympathetically.

DISSOLVE TO:

INT. LIVING ROOM—OSCAR'S APT.—NIGHT

The poker players are seated around the poker table. Speed is dealing but without much enthusiasm. Oscar is pacing and constantly looking out the window.

SPEED

Come on, Oscar. Play a few hands. It'll take your mind off Felix.

OSCAR

Then stop mentioning his name. . . . I know what you're all thinking but it's his fault, not mine. He never should have moved in here in the first place. He should have stayed with Blanche where he belonged.

CUT TO VINNIE

VINNIE

Why should he?

CUT TO OSCAR

OSCAR

Because it's his wife.

CUT TO VINNIE

VINNIE

No. Blanche is *your* wife. His wife is Frances.

OSCAR
(Pauses, looks at him)
What are you some kind of wise guy?
(He crosses to table and grabs cards out of Speed's hands)
All right, the poker game is over. I don't want to play anymore.

SPEED
Who's playing? We didn't even start.

OSCAR
(Walking near kitchen door, opening it)
I'm not going to worry about him you hear me? Why should I? He's not
worried about me. He's somewhere out on the streets sulking and crying and
having a wonderful time. . . .

CUT TO MURRAY

MURRAY
(He sniffs)
I think I smell spaghetti.

CUT TO OSCAR

OSCAR
(Very angry)
It's not spaghetti. It's linguini. *Don't you even care what's happened to Felix?*

SPEED
I thought you weren't worried.

OSCAR
Well, I'm not worried, dammit. *I'm not worried.*

The doorbell rings. A look of enormous relief comes over Oscar.

OSCAR
It's him. I bet it's him.

VINNIE
(Going to door)
I told you he'd be back.

OSCAR
(Rushes back to seat)
Play cards. Don't speak to him. I won't give him the satisfaction.
(Oscar grabs any cards and pretends to be playing)

CUT TO VINNIE

He has crossed up to front door. He turns and looks for permission. We hear Oscar's voice call, "Open the door, open the door"....
Vinnie opens the door and Gwendolyn, in a blouse and slacks, stands there. She is looking very indignant.

VINNIE
Hello.

GWEN
How do you do.
(She walks past him and into the room)

CUT TO POKER TABLE

They all seem surprised to see her. Especially Oscar. They start to get up.

OSCAR
Oh, hello, Cecily.

CUT TO GWEN

GWEN
Gwendolyn. Please don't get up, gentlemen.... May I see you for a moment, Mr. Madison?

OSCAR
(Gets up and crosses to her)
Certainly, Gwen. What's the matter?

GWEN
I think you know . . . I've come for Felix's things.

Oscar's mouth drops open and he turns in bewilderment back to the poker players. They look at each other astonished.

OSCAR
Felix? My Felix?

GWEN
Yes, that sweet, tortured man who's in my flat at this moment pouring his heart out to my sister.

CUT TO THE DOOR

Cecily, also in a blouse and slacks, rushes in.

CECILY
Gwen, Felix doesn't want to stay. Please tell him to stay.

Felix comes in right after her.

FELIX
Really, girls, this is very embarrassing. I can go to a hotel.
(To boys, sheepishly)
Hello, Vinnie.

GWEN
Nonsense. We have plenty of room on the sofa.

FELIX
But I'd be in the way. Wouldn't I be in the way?

GWEN
How could you possibly be in anyone's way?

CUT TO OSCAR

OSCAR
You want to see a typewritten list?

CUT BACK TO GWEN, CEC AND FELIX

GWEN
(looks scornfully at Oscar)
Haven't you said enough already?
(Turns to Felix)
Just for a few days.

CECILY
Until you get settled.

GWEN
Please . . . say yes.

CECILY
We'd be so happy.

FELIX
(Considers)
Well . . . maybe just for a few days.

Both girls jump up excitedly.

GWEN
Oh, wonderful.

CECILY
Marvelous.

GWEN
You get the rest of your things. We've got to clean up the house.

CECILY
And cook dinner.

GWEN
Oh, it'll be so nice having a man around the house again. Come on, Cec.

CECILY
Goodnight, gentlemen, sorry to interrupt your bridge game.

GWEN AND CECILY
Ta ta.

They both exit.

CUT TO OSCAR AND THE POKER PLAYERS

They are all standing, looking at this scene, frozen like statues.

CUT TO FELIX

He looks off at the girls and smiles.

FELIX
Ta ta.

He looks back at the players. He sighs, a note of triumph. The meek have finally inherited the earth. He crosses down the steps and across the room passing the still frozen players. He goes off to his bedroom.

SPEED
. . . What did I tell you. It's always the quiet guys.

VINNIE
(To Oscar)
Gee, what nice girls.

CUT TO HALL

Felix comes out carrying suits on hangers in cellophane protective wrapping.

ROY
Hey, Felix, are you really gonna move in with them?

FELIX
Just for a few days. Until I get my own "pad."
(He chuckles at the use of that word)

OSCAR
Hey, Felix. Aren't you going to thank me?

FELIX
(Stops)
For what?

OSCAR
For the two greatest things I ever did for you. Taking you in and throwing you out.

FELIX
(Hands suits to Oscar)
You're right, Oscar. Getting kicked out twice is enough for any man. . . .
In gratitude—
(Hand over Oscar's head)
I remove the curse.

OSCAR
(Smiles)
Oh, bless you and thank you, wicked witch of the North.

Oscar returns the suits to Felix. The phone rings and Murray picks it up.

MURRAY
Hello . . . ?

FELIX

You know, you're getting rid of me just in time. Next week I was going to make slipcovers for the furniture.
(*He laughs and starts to go*)

CLOSE-UP—MURRAY AT PHONE

MURRAY
(*Into phone*)
... Okay, just a minute.
(*Turns*)
It's your wife.

MED. SHOT—FELIX

who is standing next to Oscar.

FELIX

Oh? Well do me a favor, Murray. Tell her I can't speak to her now. But tell her I'll be calling her in a few days, because she and I have a lot to talk about. And tell her if I sound different to her, it's because I'm not the same man she kicked out three weeks ago. Tell her, Murray, tell her.
(*He looks at Oscar, proud of his new personality*)

CLOSE-UP—MURRAY

MURRAY
I will when I see her. This is Oscar's wife.

FULL SHOT—FELIX, OSCAR AND BOYS

FELIX
Oh!

Oscar crosses to phone.

FELIX
Well, so long, fellows.

Felix shakes hands with the boys.

CLOSE-UP—OSCAR ON PHONE

OSCAR
(Into phone)
Hello? Yeah, Blanche, I got a pretty good idea why you're calling. You got my checks, right? Good . . . No, I haven't been winning at the track . . . I've just been eating home a lot lately. . . .

CLOSE-UP—FELIX

Who has been watching this with pleasure. In a way he is responsible for a change in Oscar, too.

FULL SHOT—OSCAR AND FELIX

OSCAR
(On phone)
Well, Blanche, you don't have to thank me. I'm just doing what's right.

FELIX
Well, good night, Mr. Madison. If you need any heavy cleaning, I get a dollar fifty an hour.

Oscar makes a gesture to Felix not to leave yet. Felix stops on the landing next to door.

OSCAR
(On phone)
Well, kiss the kids for me. Goodnight Blanche . . . Felix!

FELIX
(Opens door)
Yeah?

OSCAR
How about next Friday night? You're not gonna break up the game, are you?

CLOSE-UP—FELIX AT DOOR

FELIX
Me? Never! Marriage may come and go, but the game must go on. . . . So
long, Frances.

He exits, closing door.

CLOSE-UP—OSCAR

OSCAR
(Smiles)
So long, Blanche. . . .

FULL SHOT—POKER TABLE

The players are all looking at this scene with enormous pleasure.

CLOSE-UP—OSCAR

OSCAR
All right. Are we just gonna sit around or are we gonna play poker?

FULL SHOT—POKER GROUP

Oscar crosses to table.

ROY
We're gonna play poker.

*There is a general hubbub as they pass out the beer, deal the cards and settle around
the table. Oscar sits.*

OSCAR
Then let's play poker.

He notices ashes on table and begins to clean them off with the palm of his hand.

OSCAR

. . . And watch your cigarettes, will you? This is my house, not a pig sty.

He cleans table as the players look at each other, stifling a chuckle.

EXT. OSCAR'S APARTMENT—LONG SHOT—NIGHT

THE CAMERA ZOOMS DOWN from the twelfth-floor window to Riverside Drive and we

FADE OUT.

THE END

The Odd Couple II

Travelin' Light

EXT. BALLPARK—DAY

On the wall of the small, sun drenched ballpark, we see that it is the home of the Sarasota Sparks, minor *minor league team. The legend on the screen tells us. . . .*

"SARASOTA, FLORIDA"
(then)
. . . . "Thirty years later."

EXT. —INSIDE THE BALLPARK

The game is in progress. The stands are filled with about 90 people, out of a possible 1,000. The batter swings and hits a slow ground ball to the shortstop, who bobbles it, picks it up to throw, drops it, picks it up again and throws ten feet over the first baseman's head. Two very old men rush for the ball.

THE PRESS BOX

OSCAR MADISON, now about seventy-four, wearing a Hawaiian shirt and a straw hat and cigar, watches in disgust. ABE, another sportswriter sits beside him. They watch the men going after the ball. One man picks it up.

OSCAR
The old cockahs in the stands are better than the young cockahs in the field.

The next batter swings and hits a foul ball into the stands.

ABE
Ooh! He just missed someone in the crowd.

OSCAR
What crowd? We could all go home in one car.

THE FIELD

The batter takes a mighty swing and misses.

THE PRESS BOX

ABE
Terrible. Maybe he should lay down a bunt.

OSCAR
This guy couldn't lay down a carpet.

THE FIELD

Batter takes a mighty swing and misses.

ABE
Now he's overswinging.

OSCAR
Don't complain. At least he's cooling off the place.

EXT. BALLPARK

Oscar and Abe walking toward the parking lot. Abe is very short, and very bald.

ABE
I always envied you, Oscar. Covering the Yankees and the Mets. I bet you
miss New York, heh?

OSCAR
Well, what was I gonna do? They were trimming costs. They sold the paper
to an Australian. Lucky the Japanese didn't buy it. It would take a year to
read the batting averages.

*A sixtyish WOMAN drives by in an open '73 Cadillac convertible. She smiles at
Oscar.*

WOMAN
(Flirtingly)
Oscar? I'm having a dinner party Friday night. We're short one man.

OSCAR
How about Abe here? He's a short man.

WOMAN
You can run, Oscar, but you can't hide.

She drives off.

OSCAR
I hate a woman who talks like Muhammad Ali.

They pass a young, attractive Hispanic COP directing traffic.

CONCHITA
Tough loss today, heh, Oscar?

OSCAR
(Big smile)
Yeah, I'm suicidal, honey. If I call 911 tonight, any chance of mouth to
mouth?

He laughs.

She laughs and shakes her head. As she turns to direct traffic, Oscar looks at her rear end.

OSCAR

Oy gutt . . . Abe? Don't you look at a good ass anymore?

ABE

If I'm not allowed to look at pastrami, why should I look at an ass?

OSCAR
(Stops at his car)
You playin' poker tonight, Abe?

ABE

I'll be a little late. I have to pay my respects. A friend in my building died.

OSCAR

What'd he die of?

ABE

He got hit by lightning on a golf course.

OSCAR

Aghh. He shoulda been using his woods. . . . Find out what his rent is. I'm always looking for cheaper.

He gets in his car and drives off, his muffler leaving a trail of dusty clouds.

EXT. TWO-STORY CONDO—EVENING

Since it's summer, it's not yet dark.

The condo is not first class but it's kept neatly by its tenants. Oscar sticks his head out of the second-floor window with a plastic bag of garbage. He looks down and lets it go.

The trash bag bounces off the rim of the garbage can and splatters everywhere.

OSCAR
I used to make that shot.

Six cats suddenly come out of nowhere and start foraging through the mess.
    A MAN about sixty-five comes out of his first-floor apartment and is aghast at the mess.

MORTON
(Angrily yells up)
Dammit, Madison. My wife and I are fed up with this. I'm filing a complaint. Are you going to clean this up??

OSCAR
Absolutely. Whatever the cats don't finish, I'll clean up later.

He goes back in.

INT. OSCAR'S KITCHEN

Obviously, it's a mess. He piles food and drinks on a tray and heads into the other room.

INT. COMBINATION LIVING ROOM AND DINING ROOM

A poker game is in session. It is five WOMEN, aged from mid-sixties to early eighties, plus Abe who is now wearing a bad toupee. Oscar enters.

OSCAR
Nobody bet. I still got a raise coming. . . . How we doing, girls?

HATTIE
Everybody's in except Esther.

ESTHER wears very thick glasses.

OSCAR
You didn't make your straight, Esther?

ESTHER
Who knows? I can't see the numbers. Why can't we play with those great big cards?

OSCAR
We tried it once. Every time I shuffled, it blew Abe's toupee off.

Abe feels his toupee.

ABE
Not anymore. This is the kind you can swim in.

OSCAR
Be careful. You swim with that rug, they'll think you're building a dam.
(He's already put down tray)
Okay, girls. Who gets the Entenmann's lemon loaf cake, no fat, no cholesterol, no taste?

MILLIE
That's mine.

OSCAR
One plate of chemical sponge cake for Millie.

He puts it in front of her. He leans over and smells WANDA's neck.

OSCAR
Wanda, you vixen. You know that perfume gets me crazy. I'd bite your neck but I don't want to get a mouthful of pearls.

WANDA
You really like it?

OSCAR
Not only do I like it, I can see I got you beat.

WANDA
(Throws in cards)
He always does that to me.

OSCAR
Don't worry about it. I lost so many brain cells today, I can't remember what
I saw.

WANDA
(To other women)
He's just like my third husband, he should rest in peace.

OSCAR
How do you know he's dead? Maybe he's just bluffing.
(Picks up plate of food)
Who gets the salt-free nachos with the cottage cheese chili?

MILLY
(A portly woman)
That's mine.

OSCAR
(Putting it down)
One Jenny Craig Mexicali Special for Senorita Abromowitz.
(He puts a glass down for Abe)
And a glass of cherry soda for Abe. Where is he?

ABE
Here.

OSCAR
Sit on a magazine, willya, I can't see you.

ABE
(Sips soda)
This isn't cherry. It's lemon.

Oscar takes a cherry out of someone's drink and drops it in Abe's glass.

OSCAR

Now it's cherry. . . . What's the bet?

FLOSSIE

Millie raised a quarter so it's thirty-three cents for you.

OSCAR

Thirty-three cents? You need nerves of steel for this game.
(He throws in money, then picks up a coin)
Hey, girls, I keep telling you. No Mickey Mouse pins from Disney World.

The phone rings. Oscar picks it up.

OSCAR
(Into phone)
Whoever it is, I'll pay you Thursday. . . . Who? . . . Brucey?
(He lights up)
Brucey, how are you, boychik?
(To girls)
Hey, girls, hold it down. It's my son from California.

ESTHER

Huh. California. My sister lost three pairs of dentures in the earthquakes.

MILLIE

So how does she eat?

ESTHER

She sends out.

OSCAR
(To phone)
No, no. It's my poker game. Last week I won a pair of earrings. . . .

INTERCUT PHONE CALL

His son BRUCEY, about thirty-two, is with an attractive girl, about thirty.

BRUCEY
You sound good, Pop.

OSCAR
You too. You still an actor?

BRUCEY
Yeah. Still an actor. I just got a call from CBS. I may get a pilot this week.

OSCAR
Terrific.
(To ladies)
Hey, my kid may get a pilot this week.

FLOSSIE
He got his own plane?

HATTIE
You don't know what a pilot is? It's a television show that doesn't get on television.

BRUCEY

BRUCEY
That's not why I'm calling, Pop. I got some big news for you.
(He looks at the girl next to him)
I'm getting married this week.
(She smiles, kisses his cheek)

OSCAR
Married? Why?

BRUCEY
Because I love her, that's why.

OSCAR
Oh. You didn't say it was a girl. . . . Listen, if you're happy, I'm happy.
(To ladies)
Hey, my kid is getting married this week.

WANDA
There goes my Rachel's last chance.

BRUCEY
It's this Sunday afternoon. Out here. You think you could come?

OSCAR
(Into phone)
Wild racehorses couldn't keep me away. Where is it?

BRUCEY
At her mother's house in San Malina. That's about two hours north of L.A.
Five in the afternoon. I'll send you the address.

OSCAR
If I'm not too nosey, sweetheart, who the hell are you marrying?

BRUCEY
Well, she's beautiful, talented, smart . . .
(HANNAH, his girl, grabs the phone)

HANNAH
(Into phone)
. . . and she loves your son.

BRUCEY
(Grabs back phone)
See what I mean?

OSCAR
I love her already. So who is she?

BRUCEY
Well . . . hold on to your hat, Pop.

OSCAR
I need a hat to hear this? . . . She's not one of those six-foot-ten basketball
players, is she?

HATTIE
What's the difference? As long as she's thin.

OSCAR
(Into phone)
I can't hear you. . . . She's whose daughter?? . . . *WHOSE???* . . . *OH, my God!!*

FELIX UNGAR—FULL-FACE CLOSE-UP

He blows his nose loudly into a Kleenex, then makes that sheep bleating sound to clear his nasal passages. Then a couple of those "Mwow Mwow!" sounds with his throat.

WE ARE IN A PLANE

Felix is sitting in economy between a MAN and a WOMAN. They look annoyed at his constant symptoms.

FELIX
(Smiles apologetically)
Sorry. Sorry.
(A STEWARDESS passes by)
Oh, Miss . . . Miss.
(She stops)
I wonder if I could change my seat? Into the nonsmoking section?

STEWARDESS
The entire plane is nonsmoking, sir. There is no one smoking on this aircraft.

FELIX
I understand. But maybe the attendants who clean out the planes in the airport were smoking in here. I'm very sensitive to that.

STEWARDESS
I'm sorry, sir. The entire plane is full.

She walks on. Felix squeezes out of his seat, excusing himself. He follows her down the aisle, then stops her.

FELIX
(*Lowers his voice*)
It's not just the smoke. The woman next to me is wearing a perfume that I have a definite allergy to.

STEWARDESS
I already moved you once.

FELIX
No, that was because of a hair spray. I know I sound crazy but I'm one of those hyper-allergenic cases. Can't you at least try?

STEWARDESS
You mean sniff every woman in the plane until you find a perfume you're not allergic to?

FELIX
Look, I didn't complain about the food, did I? I didn't eat it but I didn't complain about it.

STEWARDESS
You asked for the Hawaiian mahimahi and I told you we only serve mahimahi on west to east flights, not east to west flights.

FELIX
I just thought there was one piece of mahimahi that was making the return trip. . . . Never mind. I'll manage.

She walks away, Felix walks back and squeezes into his seat. The woman next to him looks at him as he begins to clear his throat.

WOMAN
I have some cough lozenges if you like.

FELIX
Oh, thank you very much. No. I have an unusually small windpipe. If it got stuck I could be dead in two minutes.

He smiles and shrugs. She nods. She takes out her cologne spray and sprays behind her ears lightly.

WOMAN

I hate to see someone uncomfortable.

FELIX

(He presses his finger against his left nostril so as not to breathe in the fumes. It makes him speak nasally)

No, I'm fine. A little nervous, I guess. My daughter is getting married on Sunday. Out in California. In San Ma—San Ma—Well, a friend is picking me up.

WOMAN

Oh. Congratulations.

FELIX

Thank you.

WOMAN

Are you having trouble breathing?

FELIX

Just on this side. An old sinus wound in the war. . . . Yes, she's marrying the daughter of an old friend of mine. I haven't seen him in years.

The Man on his right takes out some aftershave lotion from his case and pats some on his face. Felix looks, then presses his right finger on his right nostril, so that both nostrils are now closed.

WOMAN

So your son and his daughter have known each other before?

FELIX

(Holding nostrils, very nasal)

Not really. They grew up in different places. They met in Los Angeles. He's an actor, she's an actress.

WOMAN

Are you all right? Your face is turning bluish? Do you need oxygen?

FELIX
Yes . . .
(Points up to it)
. . . but you never know who used that before.

He starts to gag from the lack of air intake.

CUT TO:

INT. AIRPORT—DAY

Digital Readout in Baggage Claim Area. It says "Flight 91—Jacksonville"

CUT TO:

THE CAROUSEL

The bags are coming down the chute. Oscar waits right at the bottom of the chute.

CUT TO:

Digital Readout in another area of same airline. It says "Flight 96—New York"
  We see Felix waiting for his bag.

CUT TO:

OSCAR'S CAROUSEL

An old weather-beaten bag appears at the top of the carousel chute.

OSCAR
Excuse me, I see my bag. Can I get through there, please?

His bag tumbles down the chute, hits another bag and the old locks spring open. Oscar's bag is open and all its contents start to fly out.

OSCAR
(To baggage handler)
Hey! Hey! That's mishandling of luggage. That's a federal misdemeanor.

CUT TO:

FELIX'S CAROUSEL

The bags come down. Felix sees his bag. It is a neat suitcase covered with a clear plastic case around it. He picks it off and puts it down. He sees a spot on it, licks his thumb and wipes the spot off.

CUT TO:

LONG SHOT OF BAGGAGE AREA

We see Felix at one end starting to walk toward the middle where the exit to Transportation is. At the far end is Oscar, now with his clothes repacked but holding the broken bag in his arms.
  They both squint as they see each other in the distance. They both stop.

FELIX
Oscar?

OSCAR
Felix?

FELIX
(Big smile)
OSCAR!!!

OSCAR
FELIX!!!

They both start to run toward each other. After all, it's been years. They run faster and faster and just as they are about to rush into each other's arms, a woman pushing her luggage carriage pushes it in front of Felix, who goes flying into Oscar and they crash.

CUT TO:

THE CEILING

We see Oscar's clothing flying in slow motion up to the ceiling and down.

CUT TO:

EXT. AIR TERMINAL—DAY—THREE P.M.

It's where you pick up your transportation. The door from the baggage area springs open and OSCAR is pushing out a wheelchair with a disconsolate and pained FE-LIX sitting in it, his wounded leg stretched out. A porter carries their suitcases.

FELIX
We haven't even said "Hello" yet and I have a broken leg.

OSCAR
It's not broken. It's just a sprain. Hello, Felix.

They cross the road.

FELIX
Let me know when we're going to hit a bump.

They hit one. Felix bounces and winces, "AGGHH."

OSCAR
Okay. That was a bump.

CUT TO:

EXT. BUDGET RENT A CAR

Oscar comes out of Budget carrying both suitcases in one hand, a plastic box in the other and the keys to the car in his mouth. We pull back and see FELIX, standing on one leg, holding on to a post. Their car is parked in front.

FELIX

I'm supposed to give the bride away. How am I going to stand up for her on one leg?

OSCAR

You can lean on the groom. We'll work it out, Felix.

He puts the two bags down, the plastic box on top of them and puts the keys in his pocket. He helps Felix to the car, who hops on one leg.

FELIX

Maybe we can stop and get a pair of crutches somewhere.

OSCAR

I'll keep my eye open for a crutch store. I'm sure there's a lot of them on the freeway.

He props Felix up against the car, then opens the front door.

OSCAR

Okay. Now bend down and slide into the seat. Tell me when it hurts. (Felix bends slightly)

FELIX

It hurts.

He bends a little more.

FELIX

It hurts.

OSCAR
Okay. I got an idea.

FELIX
What?

OSCAR
Don't tell me when it hurts . . . because it's gonna hurt anyway. Let's do it in
one move. . . . One, two, THREE!!!

He helps FELIX into the seat.

FELIX
OW OW OW OW OW OW OW OW OW!!!
(He is in)

OSCAR
I liked "it hurts" better.

*Oscar opens the back door, throws in his bag, picks up the plastic box and rushes
around to the front and gets in. He hands Felix the plastic box.*

OSCAR
Here! I got you ice from the machine. It'll keep the swelling down.

FELIX
I need something to put the ice in.

OSCAR
Put it in your sock. What am I, an orthopedic?

*He starts the car and they pull away. As the car leaves, we see Felix's suitcase still
standing on the sidewalk.*

EXT. THE CAR

On the freeway

EXT./INT. THE CAR

We are on Felix's foot. His shoe and sock are off and his bare foot is in the box of ice. He is shivering. Felix's teeth are chattering.

OSCAR
Your foot feeling any better?

FELIX
It's not a foot anymore. It's a piece of frozen meat.

OSCAR
Hang it out the window. It's warm out.

FELIX
I'm starved. I haven't eaten since last night.

OSCAR
They didn't serve on the plane?

FELIX
No. My fish was going east.

Oscar looks at him, the same old Felix.

OSCAR
Here.
(Takes a small pack of airline nuts from his pocket)
You can have my complimentary nuts.
(Felix looks at them with disdain, he shivers)
Go on, eat 'em. If your teeth keep chattering, you'll have peanut butter in
three minutes.

FELIX
Do you know what the fat content of nuts are? Not to mention the salt
content. I could have a heart attack at the wedding.

OSCAR
(Shakes head)
I haven't seen you in what, Felix? Eight, nine years?

FELIX
(Shakes head, laughs)
Seventeen! Seventeen years. You couldn't remember we haven't seen each other in seventeen years?

OSCAR
To tell you the truth, I didn't dwell on it. . . . Okay, seventeen years and you haven't changed an iota. Your hair got whiter, your ears got bigger, your nose got longer, but you've still retained that unique, elusive pain in the ass quality that drives me besoik.

FELIX
Oh, really? Well, you *have* changed, Oscar. When I saw you in the airport, I thought you died and your mother was coming to tell me.

OSCAR
(Looks at him)
I heard that line on the *Jerry Seinfeld* show.

FELIX
So what? It's how fast I thought of it that counts.

THE CAR ON THE FREEWAY

EXT./INT. THE CAR

Felix is drying his foot with his handkerchief. He picks up box with melted water.

FELIX
Open the window, I want to throw the water out.

OSCAR
It *is* open.

Felix throws the water but the window is not open. It splashes back on Felix, who turns and looks at him.

OSCAR

Sorry. They must have just cleaned it.

EXT. THE CAR ON THE FREEWAY

EXT./INT. THE CAR

Felix is wiping the window with his sock.

OSCAR

You feeling any better? . . . Heh? . . . Whatsa matter, you sprain your tongue too?

FELIX

No. I'm angry at myself. I'm sorry I yelled at you. I behaved badly back there. I was wrong, Oscar.

OSCAR

Well, we always had bad chemistry. We mix like oil and frozen yogurt. . . . But I'm glad to see you anyway.

FELIX

Me too, Oz.
(He laughs)
God, I was a nut in those days, wasn't I?

OSCAR

From pecan to pistachio.

FELIX

I still am, I guess. I hate mess. I hate disorder. I hate how dirty the windshield on this car is . . . I went to a hypnotist to try to cure me.

OSCAR

It didn't work, right?

FELIX

No. He was late, so I straightened up his office and left.

They both laugh. Then as Felix is still laughing . . .

. . . You better get off the freeway, Oz, I gotta pee.

Oscar looks at him with murder in his eyes.

EXT. A MCDONALD'S

Oscar is sitting on an outside bench waiting for Felix. He looks at his watch. A five-year-old boy comes and looks at Oscar. He just stares at him.

OSCAR
Hi, sonny.
(No answer)
How you doin'?
(No answer. Oscar looks around)
Where's your parents?
(No answer)
You all right? You want something? What?

BOY
(Puts hand out)
Five dollars.

OSCAR
Five dollars? Why should I give you five dollars?

BOY
Your friend said you would for telling you that he's locked in the bathroom.

A disgusted look on Oscar's face as he gives the boy five dollars and heads into Mc-Donald's.

INT. THE CAR

It's on a service road.

> **OSCAR**
> Why'd you tell him five bucks? He's a kid. He'd have done it for a quarter.

> **FELIX**
> Kids don't do *anything* today for a quarter. He was wearing Michael Jordan
> sneakers that cost more than my suit.

They turn up a ramp and onto the freeway. Felix looks back.

> **FELIX**
> What freeway are we supposed to be on?

> **OSCAR**
> The 405.

> **FELIX**
> I think that sign said 101.

> **OSCAR**
> If you didn't have the brains to pee back in the airport, how the hell would
> you know what the sign said?

> **FELIX**
> *(Edgy)*
> Reading and peeing are two different things.

> **OSCAR**
> At your age, you're lucky you can do either one.

EXT. THE CAR ON THE FREEWAY

INT. THE CAR

OSCAR

Is your daughter anything like you? I mean she's not gonna clean up after the reception, is she?

FELIX

(Glares at Oscar)

My daughter's a *wonderful* girl. And your boy's lucky to get her. Let me tell you something, Oscar—

OSCAR

Felix, I don't want to fight with you. That's why I moved to Florida. If we keep this up, I'll be living in Guatemala. . . . Okay?

FELIX

Fine with me.

They drive in silence for a moment.

OSCAR

. . . So er, what are you, retired now?

FELIX

Me? Retired? Never. I do part-time charity work in a hospital.

OSCAR

What do you mean? Bed pans, things like that?

FELIX

I read books to them. I write letters. Tell 'em some jokes. It helps me too. Because ever since my last wife—well, you must have heard.

OSCAR

Yeah. I was sorry to hear about that. I heard she went very quickly.

FELIX

Yeah. She moved out while I was sleeping. Never even left a note.

OSCAR

So what is that now? Three divorces?

FELIX

Three divorces, two broken engagements and five women disappeared on the first date. Went to the ladies room and never came back.

He laughs but it hurts.

OSCAR

Well, listen, you just had bad luck with your personality.

FELIX

But I haven't given up hope, Oscar. Because I know out there, somewhere, is the right woman for me.

OSCAR

You want me to stop the car and look?

FELIX
(Smiles)

Nah ... But we should turn off here. I have to eat. It's a low sugar condition. I have to eat every four hours.

OSCAR

Then why didn't you eat when we were in McDonald's?

FELIX

Well, it wasn't time to eat yet. It was time to pee.

Oscar wants to scream.

OVERHEAD SHOT

The car swerves and passes another car to get off at the ramp, almost causing a twenty-car crack-up as all the other cars come to a screeching halt.

INT. RESTAURANT

Oscar and Felix at a table. Felix eating a salad and toast. Oscar has a cup of coffee. He takes out a piece of paper and a pen. He shoves it over to Felix.

OSCAR

Here. Make out a timetable when you eat, when you pee, when you fart, when you sleep and when you cry. Because that was the last time I'm pulling off the freeway, you hear?

FELIX

And I suppose *you* never have to pee.

OSCAR

I do it for a half hour in the morning and I'm through for the day.

Felix takes out a pill box, pours them all on the table. Starts to take them one at a time.

OSCAR

How do you know which ones to take?

FELIX

It doesn't make any difference. Whatever they fix, I got.

He swallows the pills.

OSCAR

Don't you take them with water?

FELIX

(Holds up glass of water)

Local water? From around here? You know how many pesticides they have in local water?

OSCAR

No, but lower your voice. All these people in here don't know they'll be dead
in a week.

EXT. RESTAURANT

They are walking to the car.

FELIX

Maybe we should call Hannah and tell her not to worry if we're late.

OSCAR

We won't be late. . . . So little Hannah Ungar's gonna be Hannah Madison,
heh?

FELIX

No. She wants to keep her own name. Her mother did the same thing. Very
progressive woman, you know.
(A memory comes to him)
Quite a gal, Frances was.

OSCAR

You're not gonna start grieving over your divorce again, are you? You're too
old to commit suicide. It's for younger men.

A COUNTRY ROAD. THE CAR DRIVES ALONG.

INT. THE CAR

*Felix has dozed off. He starts to cough and wakes up. Oscar is smoking what's left of
a cigar.*

FELIX

Jesus, open a window, willya?

Felix opens his window and waves the smoke out.

How long did I sleep?

OSCAR

I don't know. I didn't know you wanted me to time it.

Felix looks out the window, sees that they're in the country.

FELIX

Oh, we're off the freeway. Are we almost there?

OSCAR

I don't think so.

FELIX

You don't think so? Well, what do the directions say?

OSCAR

They're gone. I threw them out the window.

FELIX

You—you threw the directions out the *window*?? Why would you do a stupid thing like that?

OSCAR

I had them on my lap so I could read them. I lit my cigar and the hot ashes fell on my crotch, the map caught fire. I had the choice of finding the house or burning up one of the most important parts of my body. Guess which I picked?

FELIX

Why the hell didn't you wake me up?

OSCAR

I can't open a window, hold a burning map, try to steer a car sixty-five miles an hour with a lit cigar in my mouth and yell, "Oh, Felix! Would you wake up, please?"

FELIX

Unbelievable . . . So why'd you get off the freeway?

OSCAR

Because the directions said go north on 105 and then turn off on exit—and that's when the directions caught fire.

FELIX

So you just picked any exit to turn off?

OSCAR

I had to get off *someplace,* didn't I?

FELIX

This isn't *some*place. This is *no* place. . . . All right. Stop the car. I'll get the directions out of my suitcase.

Oscar jams on the brakes and the car slams to a stop. Felix glares at him, then gets out and crosses to the rear of the car. Oscar stays seated. Felix gets a funny look on his face, then comes back and looks at Oscar through the window.

FELIX

Where's my suitcase?

OSCAR

Your suitcase? In the trunk.

FELIX

No.

OSCAR

No?

FELIX

No.

OSCAR

Did you look good?

FELIX
(Holds his arms apart)
The trunk is this big. It takes a second and a half to look. *Your* 1927
cardboard suitcase is back there but not mine.

Oscar looks at him, gets out of the car, crosses to the trunk and looks.

THE TRUNK

We see Oscar's old battered suitcase but that's all.

FELIX
I'm going to try to stay very calm through the next sentence I'm going to
say. . . . If it's not in the trunk, WHERE THE HELL IS MY GOD DAMN
SUITCASE?

OSCAR
This is just a wild guess, but I'd say it's standing in front of the Budget Rent
A Car office.

FELIX
In Los Angeles?

OSCAR
That's a good guess too.

FELIX
Then why didn't you stop the car and go back?

OSCAR
Go back? It took us two hours to get to *here*. It would take us five hours to go
back there because I don't know how the hell we got *here* in the first place.
And if I *did* go back, we'd have to make three stops for you to pee, to get
locked in the john, to pay another kid another five bucks and then we'd stop
for you to eat again, take your pills and then tell me what you've been doing
with your life for the last seventeen years, does that answer your question?

Felix turns, walks away and sits under a tree and sulks. Oscar crosses to him.

OSCAR

So what'd you have in there? Two shirts, two pairs of socks, an ironing board and a tube of spot remover? I'll pay you back.

FELIX
(His eyes look up)
In that suitcase is the black afternoon formal suit I bought to wear when I give my daughter away in marriage. In that suitcase was the six-thousand-dollar silver Tiffany tray I bought as a wedding gift. In that suitcase, was ten thousand dollars in cash I intended to give to my son-in-law on *his* wedding day. Now in *your* suitcase, the police will find your broken, smashed, mutilated and dissected body in the event that you don't go back and find *my fucking suitcase. . . .*

OSCAR

Why don't we call Budget and ask them to deliver it?

FELIX

Deliver it to where? You've crisscrossed California more than the covered wagons did a hundred years ago. . . . What do we tell them? Follow the burnt pieces of directions on the freeway?

OSCAR

We'll drive to the first town we see and then we'll call Budget.

FELIX

That was my good leather suitcase. How long you think it's going to stand out there on the street, unclaimed? There's someone going to have pepperoni pizza tonight on my daughter's silver Tiffany tray.

Oscar moves back toward the car. The car is sitting on a hill.

OSCAR

Come on. Get back in the car. If it's still there, they have new things today that get them to you fast. Like Federal Express or U.P.S. or er . . . er a fax.

FELIX

Fax my suitcase? You mean I could wear a picture of my black wedding suit?
Paper copies of ten thousand dollars cash?
(He walks menacingly toward Oscar)

OSCAR

Don't get physical, Felix. I'm too old to hit but I could spit you to death.

FELIX

I just want to know why . . . why, when you get around me, you behave like
A God damn . . .
(He bangs top of car with his hand)
Idiotic. . . .
(Bangs it again)
Imbecilic. . . .
(Bangs it again)
Total moronic. . . .
(Bangs it again)
SHITHEAD????
(On shithead, he gives it one final bang)

The car slowly starts to move backward down the hill. They both stand there transfixed as it rolls faster and farther down the hill, over an embankment, crashes, catches fire and explodes. They watch it. Then Felix looks at Oscar.

FELIX

Didn't you put the brakes on?

OSCAR

Why? I didn't know you were going to punch it.

They watch it burn.

FELIX

Well, we'd better call Budget and have them fax us another car.

A BLAZING SUN

Pan down to Oscar and Felix, dragging themselves along, coats off, ties askew, sleeves rolled. They are roasting. They walk along nowhere. Some brush, a few scattered wilted trees, an arroyo but no houses or sign of life.

THE BLAZING SUN AGAIN

They stop, look up at the sun, wipe their foreheads.

OSCAR
I think I know where we are.

FELIX
You do? Where?

OSCAR
In a Clint Eastwood movie.

FELIX
"The Good, the Bad and the Stupid."

OSCAR
Hey, Felix. You're not the only one who lost everything in his suitcase.

FELIX
Really? What did you lose? An old 1967 Mets T-shirt and a half a corned-beef sandwich?

OSCAR
I lost the most important thing in my life.

FELIX
What's that?

OSCAR
My return ticket to Sarasota, Florida. . . . Instead of complaining, why don't you look for a telephone?

FELIX

You think there's a phone around here? This is where they probably test
nuclear bombs.

OSCAR

Well, they'd have to call someone to ask if they went off, wouldn't they?

FELIX

(Jumps)

Jesus! I thought that was a snake. Probably have poisonous spiders too.

OSCAR

What would they live on? You think they're gonna wait around here for two
schmucks like us to show up?

FELIX

I got to rest. Let's sit down a minute.

They sit under a dead tree, not much protection from the sun.

FELIX

Look, we have to have a plan, agreed?

OSCAR

Agreed.

FELIX

Okay. What do you think the plan should be?

OSCAR

I don't care. I agreed. I did my part.

FELIX

(Gets up)

We've got to find a phone. Then we call Hannah's mother and tell her to
send out a car to pick us up.

OSCAR

Perfect. You know her number?

FELIX
No. It was in my suitcase. We call information. Her married name now is
Frances Povitch.

OSCAR
Great. In what town?

FELIX
Er . . . San . . . San something. My daughter told me. Don't you remember?

OSCAR
I had a poker game going, I couldn't hear . . . San Marino?

FELIX
No. Not San Marino . . . San Cantino.

OSCAR
Not San Cantino . . . San Sereno.

They start to walk.

FELIX
Not San Sereno . . . San Bandino.

OSCAR
San Madina? . . . San Patina . . . San Farina?

FELIX
We could do this forever. We need a phone book. How many towns could
sound like that?

OSCAR
In California? All of them. . . . San Diego . . . San Jose . . . San Quentin . . .

*The camera is now on their backs as they walk away from us, their voices dimin-
ishing.*

FELIX

San Mateo . . .

OSCAR

San Clemente . . . Roberto Clemente . . .

FELIX

Sancho Pancho . . . Pancho Gonzales . . .

OSCAR

San Jemima.

FELIX

San *Jemima*??

OSCAR

What the hell do I know? Fernando Lamas . . . Ricardo Montalban. . . .

FELIX

Ricky Ricardo. . . .

They fade away.

A COUNTRY ROAD—DAY

Farm country, actually. It is a four-way intersection, growing crops all around. Oscar and Felix in the intersection looking in all four directions. Not a sign of life.

FELIX

(Looks up at sign pointing in all four directions)
. . . Los Pintos? Los Brisas? Los Pecos? . . . Sound familiar?

OSCAR

Yeah. They're hotels in Acapulco.

FELIX

Look, a car has to come from *some* direction. You stand here, I'll stand on the other side of the road.

OSCAR

So we can catch all the *heavy* traffic at five o'clock to Los Pecos?

FELIX

You gotta better idea, Los Idiot?

Felix crosses to the opposite side of the road. Oscar stands at the other one. They both are watching the same road from opposite directions. They're really not paying much attention to the roads that intersect them.

THE HOT SUN OVERHEAD

The two of them standing there.

FELIX

(Calls over)

You see anything yet?

OSCAR

Yeah, for a minute I thought I saw Omar Sharif on a camel.

They stand watching again. Then suddenly, seemingly out of nowhere a sports car goes whizzing by as fast as the Road Runner and disappears out of sight. . . . Oscar and Felix look at each other. Then from the opposite side of the same road, another car whizzes by even faster and out of sight, leaving a trail of dust. Oscar and Felix then move and stand on opposite sides of the road where the cars whizzed by.

Then we hear the drone of a motor. They both peer down the road. The motor gets louder.

FELIX

I hear something. You hear that?

OSCAR

With our luck, it's the Killer Bees from Brazil.

The sound becomes a roar and before they can see it, a biplane flies directly overhead and drops a load of white insecticide powder. It covers everything. When the plane leaves and the powder clears, Oscar and Felix are standing in the exact same positions, covered from head to toe with white powder.

FELIX
What the hell was that?

OSCAR
They purposely did it. They hate New Yorkers.

Felix crosses over to Oscar's side as they try, to little avail, dusting the powder off themselves.

FELIX
Who's going to pick us up now? We look like two Pillsbury doughboys.

OSCAR
Well, let's get out of the sun before we start to rise.

A HALF HOUR LATER

They are walking down the road, still very powdered. Felix suddenly starts to laugh.

OSCAR
What's funny?

FELIX
I was just thinking. If we ever get there, we could be the two figures on the wedding cake.

From behind them, we hear the engine of an old vehicle. They turn and look. It is an old fruit truck, filled with fruit, coming down the road. Oscar and Felix step to middle of the road and start waving their arms vehemently. The truck stops. The DRIVER is Hispanic, about sixty, with a short white beard and a sweet smile. Heavy accent.

DRIVER
Where you guys going?

OSCAR
San Rodondo?

FELIX
San Yolando?

DRIVER
Where??

OSCAR
San Tamale? San Taco Belle. We'll go anywhere.

EXT/INT. THE FRUIT TRUCK

The boys are in the seat next to the Driver as they move along the road.

DRIVER
(Looks at their clothes)
What you doin' out here with no car?

FELIX
Oh, that's a long story. We're going to a wedding. My daughter and his son.

DRIVER
(Big smile)
Oh, tha's nice. Then you must be very good friends.

FELIX
(With some irony)
Oh, yeah. The best . . . Look, we need to get to a telephone. Can you do that?

DRIVER
Telephone? Si. No problem. Gas station two mile from here. I take you.

FELIX
Oh. Gracias. That's very nice of you. We'd be glad to pay you.

DRIVER

No. No money. You my amigos. You poor people like me. Is my wedding gift to your children.

FELIX

You hear that, Oscar? It's a wedding gift to our children. That's more than *I'm* giving them.

Suddenly, from the opposite direction, we see a speeding, dirty old pickup truck, coming in a cloud of dust. They screech to a halt and wave to Fruit Driver, who also stops.

   Two men in the pickup. One motions to the Fruit Driver to get out and come to them. He does, then gets into a frenzied conversation with them in Spanish, which we can't hear.

FELIX
(To Oscar)

See! I told you things would work out. Everything's going to be just fine.

OSCAR

Right. I keep forgetting what a good time we've been having.

The Fruit Driver crosses back to his truck but doesn't get in.

DRIVER
(To Felix and Oscar)

Oh, very bad news. These men my cousins. They say my madre very sick. I mus' go to her very pronto. It's back where we jus' come from.

FELIX

Back there? But—

DRIVER

I go with them. They drive very fast. You take my truck to gas station. You leave it there for me. Rico. They know me.

FELIX

Are you sure? We'll be very careful with it.

DRIVER
(Crossing to other truck)
I trus' you. Adios, my compadres. You get hungry, eat some peaches.

He gets into the pickup and they speed off in a cloud of dust. Felix gets behind the steering wheel.

FELIX
(To Oscar, gloating)
Okay, compadre? I did pretty good, *comprende?*
(Oscar glares at him)
I'll drive this time, *Amigo.* Which is what I should have done in the *first* place, *muchacho!*

He puts it in gear and drives off, looking very superior.

THE ROAD

The truck ambles along, Felix driving, humming and singing . . .

FELIX
"I've got the world on a string
Sittin' on a rainbow
Ba ba da ba da my finger. . . ."

Oscar takes a bite out of a very juicy peach.

FELIX
Hey, use a handkerchief. You're getting peach juice on me.

OSCAR
You already look like a powdered doughnut. I'm adding a touch of fruit salad.

He takes another bite.

Suddenly a police helicopter appears overhead. It comes down and the OFFICER inside waves to them, motions something up ahead.

FELIX
(Smiles and waves back)
Hey, look, Os. A police helicopter. I bet Budget called them to come out and look for us.

OSCAR
How would a rental car company know we got lost?

FELIX
Maybe they found my suitcase. And anyone dumb enough to leave their suitcase is dumb enough to get lost.

He smiles and waves back. The helicopter drops lower and the Officer motions up ahead.

THE ROAD AHEAD

It's a steep incline. The truck starts to chug and puff, barely able to make it.

FELIX
Come on, baby, don't give up now. We're almost home.

OSCAR
It's not gonna make it. It's not in the cards. We're riding a dead horse and we're coming in for the funeral.

FELIX
Will you stop being such a God damn pessimist. I'm telling you we're gonna make it. I'm betting we get over that hill. . . . Come on, baby, do it for Papa.

The truck huffs and puffs. The helicopter flies on ahead and disappears. The truck climbs the hill and, finally, miraculously, gets to the very top.

FELIX

I KNEW IT!! I KNEW IT!! . . . Never count me out until the fat lady
divorces me. HA HA!!

*And down below on the other side, we see about fifteen police cars in a semicircle.
It's a roadblock. Twenty policemen behind their cars, all with handguns and rifles
pointed at the fruit truck. The helicopter lands behind them.*

FELIX

What the hell is this?

OSCAR

I don't know. Maybe they want free peaches.

THE POLICE

The lead Cop has a bullhorn.

COP

Stop the truck. Get out of the vehicle with your hands up. Lie on the ground
with your legs apart. Let's move it.

FELIX

Are they talking to us?

OSCAR

It's a weird state. Maybe cops don't go out alone here.

They get out of the truck with their hands up.

FELIX

(*To the cops*)
Officers, I think there's some mistake here.

OFFICER

On the ground, legs apart.

FELIX

We didn't steal the truck and we didn't pick the peaches, I swear.

OFFICER

ON THE GROUND, I SAID!!

They both get down on the ground. The officers rush to them and handcuff their hands behind their backs. They rush for the fruit truck.

FELIX
(To Oscar)

You don't think it's about me offering that kid money in the bathroom, do you?

The police take off the cases from the back of the truck. After the top cases are gone, we see a large tarpaulin tied down. They untie it and pull it away. Twenty illegal aliens come out with their hands up.

OFFICER
(To Felix and Oscar)

You're under arrest for violation of California Immigration Law 1407, for the transportation of illegal aliens. You have the right to remain silent.

On the ground, Oscar looks at the aliens coming out of truck with hands up.

OSCAR
(To Felix)

We could say we invited guests to the wedding.

INT. THE LOCAL JAILHOUSE

In one large holding pen are all the illegal aliens and Oscar and Felix, sitting on the floor, backs to wall. Besides the aliens, there are four or five Hell's Angels types, some shaved heads, all with lots of jewelry. They are truly mean looking. Felix chuckles to himself.

OSCAR
Something amuse you, muchacho?

FELIX
Yes. Tell me how we're going to explain to Hannah and Brucey why we were
forty years late to their wedding?

OSCAR
Stop worrying, willya? We'll get out of this.

FELIX
Not without a lawyer. Do you have a lawyer?

OSCAR
In Florida. He's ninety-two. It takes him six hours to walk to the phone, the
case'll be over. . . . We'll just tell them the truth.

Oscar looks at the BIG HELL'S ANGEL across from him.

OSCAR
You look familiar. Were you ever in sports?
(BHA nods)
I thought so. Did you play tackle for the Chicago Bears?
(BHA shakes head no)
Pro wrestling? Mr. Earthquake?
(Another no)
Then what?

BIG HELL'S ANGEL
(He's gay)
Third runner up, 1984 Olympic figure skating.

OSCAR
Right. Right. You wore a Batman costume and danced to Chopin's
Moonlight Sonata.
(The man nods)
Put on a little weight, haven't you?

BIG HELL'S ANGEL
I love sweets, what are you gonna do?

We hear the jail door open. The police usher in the Driver of the fruit truck and his two friends.
    Oscar and Felix look at each other and cross to the Driver.

FELIX
(Grabs him by his shirt)
How's your dying mother, compadre?

DRIVER
Oh, she's mucho better, gracias.

FELIX
Good. Good. I'll send her a crate of *peaches*.

OSCAR
(Angrily to driver)
Are you going to tell them the truth or not?

DRIVER
I told them. I say you picked me up on the road, gave me a ride, then I see my friends and they take me home.

OSCAR
(Looks at him, then at Felix)
. . . That's a better story than ours. I think we're in trouble.

We hear the cell door open.

POLICEMAN
(At the door)
Oscar Madison and Felix Ungar. Let's go.

Oscar and Felix get up.

FELIX
(As he leaves, he points to Driver)
If we go down, you're goin' down with us.

OSCAR
(To Felix)
What are you, Dirty Harry? You watch too much television. Let's go.

They leave the cell.

INT. DETECTIVE'S OFFICE

Felix and Oscar are sitting, detectives and an immigration official in the room.
A DETECTIVE is looking through their wallets and cards.

DETECTIVE
. . . Okay, so now tell me one more time how the rented car caught fire and
exploded.

OSCAR
He called me a shithead and punched the car. It rolled down the hill.

DETECTIVE
(To Felix)
Why'd you punch the car?

FELIX
Because the shithead threw the directions to the wedding out the window
and left my suitcase back at the car rental.

DETECTIVE
(To Oscar)
Why'd you throw the directions out the window?

OSCAR
Because they caught fire from my cigar ashes and were burning on my
crotch.

FELIX
Ha! First time he's been hot down there in years.

DETECTIVE
(Quickly on that)
Okay, boys, calm down . . . I already got a confession from the truck driver so
I have no reason to hold you. You can both go.

OSCAR
So what'd you ask us all those questions for?

DETECTIVE
It's a small town. We're starved for entertainment. . . . There's a girl outside
on the computer. Give her your family's name and she'll punch the phone
number out for you.

FELIX
Thank you.
(Picks up his wallet)

OSCAR
This is false arrest, you know. Did you call my lawyer in Sarasota?

DETECTIVE
Four times. His phone keeps ringing.

OSCAR
Well, give him a chance to get to it.

FELIX
(Grabs him)
Will you come on.

OUTSIDE OFFICE

GIRL on the computer.

COMPUTER GIRL
(To Felix)
What'd you say the name was?

FELIX

Povitch. Her married name is Frances Povitch.

The girl starts to find it on the computer.

EXT. A PRETTY COUNTRY HOUSE—DAY

We hear the phone ring inside.

FRANCES'S VOICE

Put those flowers over there, please.
(Into phone)
Hello? . . . Felix? FELIX!! We've been worried about you. Where are you?

FELIX

FELIX

Is that you, Frances? God, you sound as young as ever. . . . How's everything
going?

INT. COUNTRY HOUSE

FRANCES, late fifties, is on the phone. Wedding preparations going on behind her.

FRANCES

It's going beautifully. We thought surely we'd have heard from you by now.

FELIX

FELIX

Yeah, well, we just happened to make a wrong turn—everywhere. . . . What
city is that again?

FRANCES

FRANCES

San Malina.

FELIX

San Malina. Right. That's what I've been telling Oscar. . . .

He looks at Oscar, Oscar snarls at him.

FRANCES

FRANCES

It's 277 Poincietta Lane. Big white house as you come in town. Where are you now?

FELIX

We're in a little town called er . . .
(He snaps finger at Computer Girl)

COMPUTER GIRL

Santa Menendez.

FELIX

(Into phone)

Santa Menendez. I don't know how far that would be from you.

COMPUTER GIRL

To San Malina? About five hours.

FELIX

(Into phone)

About five hours.
(To Computer Girl)

Five *hours*??

COMPUTER GIRL

If you know the way.

FELIX

(Into phone)

Frances, they say it's going to take about five hours. . . . Well, that's a long story. . . . Right now it's . . .
(He looks at his watch)

Twenty after dust.
(He wipes face of watch)
Twenty after six . . . and we're pretty tired.
(To Computer Girl)
Is there a hotel in town?

COMPUTER GIRL

Right down the street. The Santa Florita.

FELIX

(Into phone)
Frances, Oscar and I need to get a shower, some sleep, a hot meal and we need to get our suits renovated. If we rent a car and leave here by seven in the morning, we should get there about noon. Plenty of time.

FRANCES

FRANCES

All right, Felix. Drive carefully.

FELIX

We will. . . . No, thanks. There's nothing you can do.

OSCAR

The suitcase.

FELIX

(Into phone)
Well, I do need a favor. Could you call Budget Rent A Car at the L.A. airport? I left my suitcase there. Maybe they could send it out to your house. . . . Oh, that would be a big help. See you tomorrow. Bye. . . .

He hangs up. There is a look of sadness on his face, of things lost. Then he snaps out of it. To Oscar as he starts for the door.

Come on. We're going to the Santa Florita Hotel.

OSCAR

Did you get directions?

As he follows him out.

INT. HOTEL ROOM

It's a single room with a double bed. Oscar is walking back and forth in his underwear and socks. We hear the shower going in the bathroom and Felix humming and singing happily. Oscar knocks on the door.

OSCAR
(Loudly)

How long you gonna be in there? That's local water, you know. Keep your mouth shut.

The shower stops, the door opens. Felix leans out, all wet, towel draped around him.

FELIX

Did the kid pick up our suits to be cleaned?

OSCAR

Yeah. He was still coughing as he left.

FELIX

And did you give him money to buy underwear and socks?

OSCAR

Yes.

FELIX

Did he think it was weird?

OSCAR

No. He looked like he did it all the time.

There's a knock on the door. Felix goes back in to dry off. Oscar crosses and opens the door. The BELLMAN, no uniform. He hands Oscar a brown paper bag.

242

BELLMAN

Here's your socks and underwear. I got the right sizes. Your suits'll be back
in a half hour.

OSCAR
(Takes the bag)
Thanks.
(The Bellman waits)
I'll have to get you later. I don't have any change in my shorts.

He closes the door.

Felix! Our new underwear arrived.

FLIP SCREEN

*We see Felix and Oscar looking at themselves in the mirror. As we pan down, we see
their underwear. Oscar's undershirt is army khaki and his shorts have pictures of fish
and hunting dogs. Felix's undershirt is light purple and his shorts have pictures of
Elvis Presley.*

FELIX
(Aghast)
Where'd he buy this? At Graceland?

OSCAR

It's Santa Menendez, for crise sakes. The Georgio Armani boutique must
have been closed.

INT. RESTAURANT IN THE HOTEL—NIGHT

*Felix and Oscar enter in their cleaned suits, shirts and ties. It's a very rural restau-
rant. Lots of truckers and farmers at the bar and at the tables. The television over the
bar is showing the country-western* Dancing Partners *show.*
A heavy WAITRESS comes over with some menus.

WAITRESS
Hi, there. Drinks or dinner?

OSCAR
(Smiles)
Does one preclude the other?

FELIX
We'll have a drink at the bar before we eat, thanks.

WAITRESS
Just let me know when you're ready.

She leaves. As Oscar and Felix cross to the bar, everyone there turns to look at them.
Looks like rough trade.

FELIX
(Aside to Oscar)
I don't think this is our kind of crowd.

OSCAR
(Aside)
If anyone gets tough, show 'em your underwear.

They sit at the bar. BARTENDER crosses to them.

BARTENDER
What'll it be?

FELIX
I'll have a dry martini on the rocks, please.

BARTENDER
Martini?

The other men down the bar turn to see who ordered a martini. Felix smiles at them.

OSCAR
Double scotch for me.

The bartender nods and leaves. Oscar smiles at the boys down the bar.
We hear a WOMAN's voice to their left.

WOMAN'S VOICE
A couple of beers here, please.

Felix and Oscar turn.
TWO WOMEN in jeans and T-shirts, both about forty-five or so, but with good figures and not bad looking, in a Harley Davidson sort of way, sit and open a pack of cigarettes. Oscar nudges Felix and smiles at the ladies.

OSCAR
'Evening.

FIRST WOMAN
Hi.

OSCAR
Beautiful weather, isn't it?

FIRST WOMAN
Just terrific, honey.

She smokes and drinks. Oscar turns and gives Felix one of those "look what we just met" looks.

FELIX
(Aside)
If you're thinking what I *think* you're thinking, just *forget* it.

OSCAR
(Aside)
I'm not thinking. I'm just talking.
(He turns to girls)
Nice town you have here, ladies.

SECOND WOMAN
It's not our town, Pops. Just passin' through.

OSCAR
Really. So are we. Where you headin'?

FIRST WOMAN
Don't know yet. Maybe Lake Tahoe, maybe Vegas. Who knows?

OSCAR
Just lovers of the open road, eh? . . . Oh. This is my friend Felix. They call me Oscar.

FIRST WOMAN
Hi, Felix. Hi, Oscar. I'm Thelma.

OSCAR
Thelma?
(To Second Woman)
You're not Louise, are you?

SECOND WOMAN
Like I haven't been asked *that* a million times . . . I'm Holly.

OSCAR
Holly? Very nice name. Especially around Christmas.

He laughs. The girls smile, amused. Felix is miserable.

HOLLY
Cute.

OSCAR
Like you haven't heard *that* line a million times.
(He's still chuckling)
So, er, are you ladies staying here at the hotel?

THELMA
We're savin' our money for Tahoe. We got a van out back.

OSCAR

A van? Really? That couldn't be all that comfortable to *sleep* in, could it?

THELMA

Now, Oscar. If I didn't know better, I'd say a nice old grandfather like you was trying to hit on a couple of young ladies.

OSCAR

In the first place, I'm not a grandfather. And I'm not as old as I look. I had some plastic surgery done recently and this quack doctor botched it up.

Felix chokes on his drink. Oscar starts pounding his back, then smiles at the girls.

HOLLY

Your friend doesn't talk much, does he?

OSCAR

No. He's the doctor who botched it up.

This really breaks the girls up. Oscar laughs and rubs Felix's back.

You okay, Doc?

THELMA
(Still laughing)
You know, with all the dead honchos around here, you're the only fun guy around.

The Waitress comes over to Oscar.

WAITRESS

Excuse me, but we're closing the kitchen in a half hour, if you still want to eat dinner.

OSCAR

Closing the kitchen?
(He looks at his watch)
My God, is it eight o'clock already? Where did the time go?

FELIX
(Gets off the stool)
If you ladies will excuse us, we haven't eaten all day. Come on, Oscar.
Doctor's orders.

He starts to move away. Oscar grabs his arm.

OSCAR
Where's your manners, Felix? Perhaps the ladies would like to join us before
they retire to their van.

FELIX
They said the kitchen was closing soon. Maybe they don't have that much
food.

OSCAR
Then we'll share.
(To ladies)
Ladies, would you give us the pleasure of your delightful company for a light
supper.

THELMA
(Looks at Holly)
You think we can trust these guys?

HOLLY
If not them, then who? . . . We'll freshen up. See you at the table.

*They go. Oscar watches their tight buns in their tight jeans. Felix and Oscar start for
the table.*

FELIX
Are you *crazy?* Two middle-aged bikers? They're tougher than the guys we
left in jail. And have you ever stopped to think of what we could get?

OSCAR
Lucky is the only word that comes to mind.

FELIX
Well, I'm not letting you do this. To either of us.

OSCAR
I know it's not going to happen. They'd never even come up to our room. And it would take two years for you and me to climb into their van. . . . And the last thing I'd want them to see is our underwear.

FELIX
Then what are you doing this for?

OSCAR
To be wanted. To get close to it happening one more time. The wick is almost out, Felix. All I want is for the candle to glow rather than curse the darkness.

FELIX
It's not going out, Oscar. Not yours and not mine. But I still have hope that out there, somewhere, we'll find the right lamplighter.

OSCAR
We just used so many metaphors, I forgot what the hell we were talking about.

An ELDERLY MAN, about eighty-four, neatly dressed in a very nice suit, with a sweet face and kind disposition, sits at the table next to them. He takes the napkin and tucks it under his chin and looks at the menu.

ELDERLY MAN
Good evening.

FELIX
(Smiles)
Good evening.

ELDERLY MAN
You gentlemen here for the seminar?

FELIX
What seminar is that?

ELDERLY MAN
"Life. Does it Really Have to End?" . . . Dr. John Boxer, a wonderful man. I come up here every year for it. People younger than you gentlemen flock to hear him. I'm eighty-six myself and Dr. Boxer sees no reason why I can't be around to celebrate the year two thousand and twenty. Maybe more.

FELIX
Isn't that interesting. Well, you certainly don't look eighty-six.

ELDERLY MAN
Thank you. A minimum of exercise, a maximum of clean living. Last day of the seminar tomorrow but I've got to get back home to San Malina. My youngest daughter's sixty-third birthday.

Felix and Oscar look at each other.

OSCAR
San Malina? That's where we're going. Our two kids are getting married there.

ELDERLY MAN
Fancy that. Do you gentlemen need a lift?

FELIX
Well, actually we could. . . . We hear it's a five-hour drive.

ELDERLY MAN
Nonsense. I know every road and byroad. You come with me. I'll have you there in less than two hours. We leave six A.M. on the dot.

FELIX
. . . What do you think, Oscar?

OSCAR

Six o'clock? Gee, that's a little early for me. I may have some business tonight with friends from *Lake Tahoe*.

Felix throws him an angry glance.

ELDERLY MAN

You'll never live a long life sleeping late. You meet me out front six A.M. and we'll be on the road. I have a Rolls Royce. Very comfortable auto.

FELIX

Sounds great to me.

ELDERLY MAN

You seem like fine men. Well bred. Otherwise I wouldn't ask you.

Thelma and Holly arrive at the table wearing more make-up, puffing away. As they sit . . .

THELMA

Can you imagine these creeps closed the bar already?
(She takes out a pint bottle from hip pocket)
Well, don't worry, honey. I stay open all night.

HOLLY

(Squeezes next to Felix)
We just took a vote about you guys in the john. You won in a landslide.

They laugh it up. Felix looks at the Elderly Man with a feeble smile. The old man takes his napkin off.

ELDERLY MAN

Perhaps I was wrong. Six A.M. *would* be a little early for men like you.
(He gets up)
Good evening.
(Nods to girls)
Ladies.

He goes. Felix jumps up.

FELIX
(To Oscar)
You go to Tahoe. I'm going in a Rolls Royce.
(Turns, goes, calling off)
Sir! Sir! May I speak to you for just a second.

He is gone. Oscar is alone with the girls.

THELMA
Bummer. . . . What are two wide awake girls gonna do with one hunky
funny guy?

OSCAR
Why don't we all write a suggestion on a piece of paper?

*All three laugh. Then Holly puts her two end fingers in her mouth and whistles
loudly to the bartender.*

HOLLY
(Calls out)
A little music here wouldn't kill you, would it?

OSCAR
I've tried to whistle like that. I could never do it.

HOLLY
It's all in the fingers. I'll lend you mine later.

*The girls laugh, he finishes his drink in one gulp. The music comes on. It's Tony
Bennett singing one of his classic love songs. (Not "San Francisco").*

THELMA
Now Tony Bennedetto's over seventy and he's still hot.

HOLLY
(Looks over her shoulder)
I wish your cute little boy scout friend would come back. I'm just itching to dance.

OSCAR
(Gets up)
I'll get him. Don't scratch yet.

He runs off. While they wait, the two girls sing the lyrics along with Tony Bennett.

LOBBY

Which is small. Felix is on a house phone as Oscar runs over.

FELIX
(Into phone)
Yes, sir. I'll be outside at six A.M. sharp. Thank you very much, sir.
(He hangs up. To Oscar)
I'm going in the Rolls Royce.

OSCAR
I'll go with you. I promise. Just do me one favor. Come back inside and dance for me.

FELIX
Why would I want to dance for you?

OSCAR
Because I'm hunky and the other one's itchy . . . Felix, please. Just come in and dance and you can call all the shots the rest of the way.

INT. THE DINING ROOM

We are on the light fixture above. Tony B. is singing something else. Pan down and Oscar is dancing very close with Thelma, pan over and Felix is dancing closer to Holly than he'd like.

HOLLY

Loosen up a little, honey.

FELIX

I'm trying. I think I'm stuck on your velcro.

She does a twirl around him, then back close to him.

HOLLY

I went to high school with a boy like you.

FELIX

Yeah? Who *was* he, the principal?

Pan over to Oscar and Thelma.

THELMA

You are a *very* good dancer. . . . Don't you think?

OSCAR

I don't know. I never looked down.

She does a few fancy steps, then back close to him.

THELMA

Let me try a new step on you.
(She leads him, then does a double dip)
You got it, honey?

OSCAR

Very good. What do you call that?

THELMA

Safe sex.

The phone rings at the bar. The bartender picks it up.

BARTENDER
(Into phone)
Yeah? ... Who? ... Just a minute.
(Hand over phone, he calls out)
Someone wants to know if a Thelma and Holly are here.

THELMA
What does he sound like?

BARTENDER
Drunk and *real* mad.

THELMA
(To Oscar)
Have to run, Hon. Don't ask questions.

HOLLY
(To Felix, as she runs for her jacket)
You never met me, you never saw me and you never danced with me.

They both grab their jackets and dart out the back way. Oscar and Felix stand there alone.

FELIX
Okay. Are you satisfied?

OSCAR
(Dour)
Satisfied is not how I would describe it.

INT. THE BOYS' BEDROOM—NIGHT

Both undressing, taking off their pants.

FELIX
I call the shots now, right?

OSCAR
Right.

FELIX
(Near the wall switch)
Ready for lights out?

OSCAR
Ready.

Felix turns out the lights. The room is dark but their undershorts keep glowing in the dark.

FELIX
Either these are the ugliest shorts ever made, or this town was hit by a nuclear disaster.

EXT. FRONT OF HOTEL—SIX A.M.

Felix and Oscar waiting. Oscar shields his eyes from the rising sun. We hear the sound of a car horn tooting.

FELIX
(Turns, looks)
Will you get a load of this thing.

We see the car coming. It is a large 1954 Rolls Royce.

FELIX
How about that?

OSCAR
Probably gets two blocks to the gallon.

The car stops. Elderly Man at the wheel.

ELDERLY MAN
Glad to see you both could make it. Climb in, boys.

They get in. Felix in front. Oscar in the back.

ELDERLY MAN
There's only four of these cars left in America and I own them all.

FELIX
Oh? You're a collector?

ELDERLY MAN
No. I use the other three for parts. Hang on to your hats, boys.

And they drive off. About twelve miles an hour.

THE ROAD

The Rolls Royce moves slowly on.

IN THE CAR

OSCAR
Is this as fast as it goes?

ELDERLY MAN
It takes a few minutes to warm up, then we ride like the wind.

EXT. ROAD

The car is still doing about twelve miles per hour.

IN THE CAR

OSCAR
(*Looks at his watch*)
It's been a half hour. And the wind is going faster than us.

ELDERLY MAN
It just seems that way. Actually we're doing eighty-five right now.
(He points to dashboard)

FELIX
(Looks at dashboard)
No, sir. That's your clock. It says eight twenty-five.

ELDERLY MAN
Oh, don't mind that clock. It always breaks down.

FELIX
No offense, sir, but do you really think we'll make it to San Malina in two
hours?

ELDERLY MAN
Who said that?

FELIX
You did. Last night.

ELDERLY MAN
No, no. I think you misunderstood me. What I meant was, I can make this
five-hour drive *seem* like two hours.

Felix and Oscar look at each other. They're in trouble.

. . . Take in the scenery. Relax and enjoy being alive and well. Doing that, I
actually once made it back in an hour twenty.

Oscar and Felix sink back in their seats, in trouble again.

EXT. THE ROAD

*The Rolls Royce creeps along as cars honk and pass them, a school bus passes them,
five bikers pass them and four hikers pass them.*

OSCAR
The only thing that hasn't passed us was that McDonald's back there.

FELIX
(To Elderly Man)
With all due respect, at this rate we're going to be late to our kids' wedding.
Could you possibly let us off at the next town so we can rent a car?

ELDERLY MAN
Well, I'll be sorry to lose your company, but if that's what you want. Santo
Yosanto is just thirty miles from here.

FELIX
Santo Yosanto?

ELDERLY MAN
We'll be there in no time at all.

OSCAR
Nothing faster than that?

The Elderly Man yawns.

ELDERLY MAN
Excuse me, but the scent of the trees and flowers always intoxicates me.

FELIX
Look, if you're intoxicated, I'd gladly be your designated driver.

ELDERLY MAN
No, no. I'm fine.
(He yawns again. The car bumps)
Good gracious. Did I just hit a rabbit on the road?

Felix looks out window. We see a rabbit just looking at them.

FELIX
Yes, sir. But at this speed, he hardly felt it.

ELDERLY MAN
Well, we'll be home soon enough.

EXT. THE ROAD

The car seems to be slowing down . . . slower and slower . . . until it comes to a stop, right there in the road.

EXT./INT. CAR

OSCAR
(Looks around)
Why are we stopping here?

FELIX
(Nudges Elderly Man)
Sir, you've stopped in the middle of the road. That's a very dangerous thing to—are you all right?
(He nudges him again. No response)
Jesus, I think he's asleep.

OSCAR
Why? When was he awake? . . . All right, move him aside and I'll drive.

Felix feels the old man's pulse.

What are you waiting for? He'll wake up and then *snails* will start passing us.

FELIX
He's not *going* to wake up. He's dead.

OSCAR
Dead??? How do you know?

FELIX
No pulse and no heartbeat means dead. I've seen this in the hospital.

OSCAR

Seen what? All you did was read books and tell jokes.

FELIX

What do you want me to do, an autopsy? He's dead I'm telling you. . . . At least he went quickly.

OSCAR

You call twelve miles an hour quickly? . . . What are we gonna do with him?

FELIX

What do you mean?

OSCAR

He knows the directions. We don't. It would take us two days to get there. And without camphor balls, it would not be a pleasant trip.

FELIX

Let me think.

The body's weight suddenly falls to the left and his head is out the side window.

OSCAR

Well, while you're thinking, pull him back in before a bird sits on his head.

FELIX

Jeez!
(He turns to reach over and suddenly screams and grabs his neck)
Oh, my neck! I strained my neck. Dammit! This *always* happens.

OSCAR

Always? You mean whenever you try to pull a dead body back in?

FELIX

Will you get out and push his head back in, for crise sakes. I can't move.

Because a car drives by and honks, Oscar gets out on the road side, so as not to get hit. As he's outside, a huge truck whizzes by and the wind blows the toupee off the dead man. Oscar doesn't see it as he comes around the car so that now he sees the dead man with no hair.

OSCAR

Hey! This guy is starting to decompose already.

FELIX

His hairpiece flew off. Go back and get it.

OSCAR

Why? He's dead. Who does he have to look good for?

FELIX

Out of respect. Maybe his family never knew. Just go get it.

Oscar goes back. The hairpiece is about ten yards away. Suddenly a bird flies down and sits on it.

Oscar goes back. The bird doesn't move.

OSCAR
(Calls out)
Felix!

FELIX
(Holding his neck)
What?

OSCAR

It's not a hairpiece anymore. Now it's a nest.

FELIX
(Turns painfully)
Well, shoo him away.

OSCAR

Shoo! . . . Shoo!
(The bird still doesn't move. To Felix)
He doesn't know what shoo means.

FELIX
Well, flap your arms. Do I have to do everything?

Oscar flaps his arms and yells "Shoo! Shoo!" The bird flies off but takes the hairpiece with it in its beak.

OSCAR
(*Looking up*)
Well, unless that bird flies south to Sarasota, we'll never see that again.

A bigger truck whizzes by this time and the strong wind blows the Elderly Man back in the car, but his head falls on Felix's lap. Oscar goes back around the car and gets in the back seat again. All he can see is Felix.

OSCAR
Where'd he go?

FELIX
He's in my lap.

Oscar leans over and looks.

OSCAR
That's not a good position. Because it looks like—

FELIX
I *KNOW* what it looks like. . . . Help me pull him up.

Oscar reaches over and the two of them straighten him up. We suddenly hear a gunshot from in the woods.

OSCAR
What the hell is that?

FELIX
Sounded like a gunshot. Maybe it's hunting season.

OSCAR
What kind of animals would they have around here?

We hear another gunshot. Then the bird, now dead, bounces off the hood of the car but the hairpiece stays on the windshield.

FELIX
Can you believe this? . . . Go out and get it.

OSCAR
In the last three minutes, I've walked more than we've driven today.

He goes out to get hairpiece. As he leans over the hood of the car the body falls forward, his head hitting the horn. The horn blasts out loudly. Oscar yells and jumps.

OSCAR
Are you crazy??

FELIX
I didn't do it. *He* did it.

OSCAR
Well, check his pulse again.

He comes around and gets back in the back seat, holding the hairpiece.

OSCAR
Here. You take it.

FELIX
I don't want it. Put it on his head.

Oscar puts the hairpiece on his head but puts it on backward. Felix looks at the body.

FELIX
You got it on backwards.

OSCAR

Oh. For a minute I thought he was looking at me.

He turns the hairpiece around, then pushes it down to make sure it sticks. Felix reaches into the dead man's pocket, starts to feel around.

OSCAR

What are you doing?

FELIX

I've got to get his name and address, don't I? So we can call his family.

He takes out wallet, opens it up.

FELIX
(Reads)

Adam Beaumont . . . Beaumont? . . . I've heard of him. Owns half of northern California. Oscar, this is one of the richest men out here.

OSCAR

Doesn't spend much on toupees, does he? . . . We're wasting time here. What if the police show up?

FELIX

We don't have to worry about that anymore.

OSCAR

Why not?

FELIX

Because they just pulled up behind us.

Oscar turns and looks. We see a California state trooper car behind them. It stops, two OFFICERS get out of the car and approach the Rolls.

OSCAR

This should be interesting.

The body falls to the right again, his head leaning against Felix's shoulder. The hair-piece falls off and Felix picks it up.

OFFICER

(At their window)

Don't you know you can't stop in the middle of a road. Pull the vehicle over, please.

FELIX

Well, we'd have to move the driver first and as you can see—

OFFICER

Is he sick?

FELIX

No.

OFFICER

Is he drunk?

FELIX

No . . . try dead.

The Officer looks at Felix, then takes the pulse of Mr. Beaumont.

OFFICER

How'd this happen?

OSCAR

We don't know. We think God just came and took him.

FELIX

He was eighty-six years old. He just gave us a lift.

OFFICER
What's that in your hand, sir?

FELIX
This is his hairpiece. It won't stay on.

OFFICER
I mean in your other hand.

FELIX
(Looks at wallet)
This? Oh. It's his wallet. We were looking for his address so we could take him home.

Both Officers draw their guns quickly and aim them.

OFFICER
I'm going to ask you two to step out of the car, please.

FELIX
That's all we've been doing on this trip.

They both get out, their hands up.

OFFICER
Just face forward and place your hands against the car, please.
(They do it)
Keep your legs apart while we search for identification.

He holds the gun on them while the other cop searches them.

OFFICER
You both have the right to remain silent.

FELIX
(Glares at Oscar)
All this because you left my suitcase at the car rental.

INT. POLICE DEPARTMENT—SANTA MENENDEZ

They are in the same room, sitting in the same chairs, looking at the same Detectives. The first Detective is looking through Mr. Beaumont's wallet.

DETECTIVE

. . . So the man is dead, you have his wallet, riding in an antique car worth over a hundred and fifty thousand dollars . . . How do you think this looks?

OSCAR

Well, to you it looks terrible. To my mother, she wouldn't be all that upset.

FELIX

Look, we didn't kill him, and we didn't rob him. . . . You believed us before, why don't you believe us now?

DETECTIVE

Because I didn't expect you to keep bouncing back in here like a beach ball . . . Why did you take his toupee?

FELIX

We didn't. A truck whizzed by and blew it off.

OSCAR

I tried to get it back but a bird sat on it. I shooed him and he flew away with the hairpiece.

DETECTIVE

You shot him? You had a gun?

OSCAR

No. I *shooed* him.
(He flaps his arms)
Shoo! Shoo! . . . Then a hunter shot him and he fell down on the car and the hairpiece fell on the windshield.

The Detective stares at him suspiciously.

... I hope there's not going to be a trial because I would hate to repeat that story in court.

Another officer comes in, whispers in the Detective's ear, who nods.

DETECTIVE

All right ... examination reveals he died of natural causes. His daughter just informed us that he called last night and said he was going to give a lift home to two nice men he met at the hotel. . . . So once again, you're out of here.

They get up, taking their wallets off table again.

DETECTIVE

But if I see you two back here under arrest, I will charge you both with disturbing the law. There's a bus that leaves here in twenty minutes. They make a quick stopover in San Malina. Be on it! Get off it! And stay out of my face. Got it?

EXT. A BUS ON THE ROAD

In the bus. Felix and Oscar sitting on the bus.

FELIX
(In window seat)
... Oscar, I'm going to say something now that's going to surprise you.

OSCAR

Why do you always have to introduce everything you're going to say? It's either "Oscar, let me tell you something," or "Oscar, you may not like this but I'm going to say it anyway." . . . Why don't you just say it, get it over with, then I can read a magazine and you can start thinking of the next thing you're going to say. . . . What is it?

FELIX
... I actually had a good time on this trip.

OSCAR

You did? As much as World War Two?

FELIX

I mean it. Sure it was dirty and scary and ugly and expensive. But I met a lot
of people I never would have met before. I got out of the house. Had an
adventure. That there's more to life than a job, a dinner alone and a TV
show. I wasn't involved with my own problems every minute. I actually feel
younger now than I have in years.

OSCAR

Why didn't you say this last night when we could have used it?

EXT. THE BUS ON THE ROAD

It is traveling at a good pace.

EXT./INT. THE BUS

Felix and Oscar are both asleep in their seats.

THE ROAD

*The BUS DRIVER, African American, looks down the road, then squints, wonder-
ing what he's seeing.*

UP AHEAD

*Two men, mid-forties, both rough types, stand brazenly in the middle of the lane the
bus is driving on, their hands on their hips. As the bus gets closer, they pull out guns
from the back of their belts and take dead aim on the driver.*

BUS DRIVER

What the hell . . . ?

*He hits the brakes and the bus comes to a screeching, sliding stop. Bags and packages
fall from the racks overhead. LEROY bangs on the bus door with his gun. The
driver opens it. The two gunmen jump on the bus. They are LeRoy and JAYJAY.*

LEROY

All right, everyone stay put. This ain't no robbery.

They move slowly up the aisle, checking out everyone. Oscar and Felix look at them, then at each other, puzzled. LeRoy and JayJay finally get to Oscar and Felix, glare at them. The boys smile back. The gunmen then step to the row directly behind Oscar and Felix.

    Two women pretend to be asleep, jackets pulled up over them. LeRoy stops, then pulls the jackets off. It is Thelma and Holly.

LEROY

I told you, Thelma, if you ever left me, I'd come 'n get you. Now move your ass, l'il darlin'.

THELMA

The hell I will.

Oscar and Felix turn, see the two girls. They look shocked, then try to slip down in their seats.

JAYJAY

Holly, you tryin' to break my heart? Runnin' off with someone else?

HOLLY

I told you, JayJay. I ain't takin' your crap no more.

OSCAR
(Aside to Felix)
Remember, we don't know them, we've never seen them.

JAYJAY
(To Oscar, quickly)
What'd you say?

OSCAR

I honestly can't remember.

LEROY
(To Thelma, pointing to Oscar and Felix)
That's them, ain't it? Bartender at the hotel described them.

JAYJAY
(To Oscar and Felix)
What happened to that big old Rolls Royce you boys had this mornin'?

FELIX
I think you're mistaking us for another gentleman who's dead.

LeRoy grabs Thelma by the wrist and yanks her out of the seat. Then he pulls Holly out as well.

LEROY
Let's go, girls. We're *all* goin' home.

JAYJAY
(Points gun at Oscar and Felix)
That means you too, boys.

OSCAR
You're taking us home?

JayJay puts gun right at them, then motions for them to get up and go. They do. LeRoy pushes Thelma and Holly ahead of them. JayJay prods Oscar and Felix.

FELIX
(Aside)
Do something. Say something.

OSCAR
ATTICA! ATTICA!
(To Felix)
That's all I could think of.

They all move out of the bus except LeRoy, who turns to all the passengers.

LEROY

These men were abducting our wives. Wouldn't any man here do the same as us?

He gets off. They all pile into the open convertible, then drive off quickly, making a screeching U-turn on the road and heading back home.

THE BUS

The Driver picks up the radio phone.

DRIVER

Alice? Call the police. We just had a double abduction here.

THE ROAD

In the convertible, LeRoy drives with the two girls up front. JayJay has Oscar and Felix in the back.

FELIX

Look, we just had an innocent drink and an innocent couple of dances with the girls. . . . It was all very innocent.

OSCAR
(Aside)
Get off the innocent thing.

FELIX
(Laughs)
But run off with them? No . . . I mean, why would two beautiful women like these run off with two old geezers like us?

JAYJAY
When the goose wants it, the geese come runnin'.

FELIX
(Stares at him, bewildered)
. . . No. Not geese. *Geezers.* We're *Geezers,* not geese.

OSCAR
(To JayJay)
Ask them yourself. . . . Ladies, did we abduct you?

THELMA
Honey, there's no way these two jackasses are gonna believe me and Holly.

JAYJAY
Where you wanna stop, LeRoy?

LEROY
Just other side of this hill there's a nice stretch of woods. That'll do fine.

FELIX
Do fine? Do fine for what?

JAYJAY
(Smiles)
To cook us a couple of fine geezers.

LeRoy and JayJay laugh. Then Thelma and Holly laugh.

HOLLY
That's funny.
(Turns to Oscar and Felix)
I'm sorry, fellas, but that just strikes me funny.

Oscar and Felix look at each other.

OSCAR
(To Felix)
You had to bring up geezers, heh?

The car comes to the crest of the hill and just as it starts down, we see six police cars blocking the road with twelve cops all pointing their guns at LeRoy's car.

LEROY
God dammit to hell!!

OSCAR

Don't worry about it. I know all of them personally.

INT. THE POLICE ROOM

The same room, the same chairs, the same Detective.

The Detective has his head in his hands, his elbows on the desk. He is disconsolate. Felix sits, looking at the floor. Oscar sits staring at the ceiling. The second burly Detective stands and just watches this.... It is quiet for a long time.... Finally—

FELIX

(To Detective)

—Don't you even want to talk about it?

DETECTIVE

(Only his eyes look up)

No.

FELIX

... Ever??

DETECTIVE

What's the point? No matter what I say, you two still end up in here.

OSCAR

(Aside to second Detective)

Would it be possible to find out the results of the second race at Hollywood Park? I've got a trifecta going.

SECOND DETECTIVE

A what?

OSCAR

A trifecta. You've got to pick the three winning horses in the exact order that they finished.

FELIX

I don't believe this. We've got a wedding we can't get to and all he has on his mind is a *trifecta*.

DETECTIVE
(Looks at Oscar)
I'll tell you who won.

OSCAR
You know?

DETECTIVE
Yes . . . *I* won. You're my trifecta. The same two men have been arrested
three times, for *three* different crimes, and all *three* times by my men. In less
than fourteen hours. You know what the odds are on that happening? In any
police station in the world?

OSCAR
Roughly, I'd say twelve million to one.

DETECTIVE
And what would it be if it happened in a small sheriff's office in a little town
called Santa Menendez, California?

OSCAR
It would be in the trillions. No bookie could handle it.

FELIX
Oscar, of all the differences we've ever had, of all the fights we've ever had, of
all the petty arguments we've ever had—

OSCAR
(To Detective)
We can keep on talking 'cause he'll be on this a half hour.

FELIX
—of all the times I wanted to choke you by the throat, this is the worst. . . . If
you say trifecta one more time, I'm going to choke you until you're dead, and
he can arrest me one more time, for one more crime, and one more time in
his office. Then he'll have a FOUR-FECTA!! So SHUT THE FUCK UP,
OKAY???

OSCAR

That would be the biggest payoff in the world.

FELIX

What would?

OSCAR

A four-fecta. There isn't a racetrack in the world that—

Felix jumps out of his chair and goes for Oscar's throat, but the second Detective grabs him and holds him back.

DETECTIVE

Sit down! Both of you! . . .
(They sit)
Okay. Since the ladies already gave a statement that you two had nothing to do with the abduction, I have no reason to hold you.

FELIX

Then why are we here?

DETECTIVE

Because if I let you go, I'm afraid you'll come back. . . . I'm running for sheriff next year and I can't run on a campaign of mostly arresting you two.

OSCAR

I wouldn't advise it.

DETECTIVE

If I promise to get you to San Malina in time for the wedding, I need your guarantee that you'll never come within a hundred miles of this town. No. *Two* hundred. . . . Make it three.

FELIX

You've got my solemn oath.

OSCAR

Since I've only been here once in seventy-four years, the odds on my coming back—

FELIX

Don't finish that sentence, Oscar.

DETECTIVE

(Putting on his jacket)

All right, let's go.

FELIX

The wedding's at four. How will you get us there on time?

DETECTIVE

Leave that to me.

They all start to leave.

OSCAR

I wish you had subways out here. I never got lost on subways. . . .

INT. LOBBY OF POLICE STATION

At the far end, we see Thelma and Holly embracing and kissing their respective spouses.

FELIX

They made up?

DETECTIVE

Yeah. The boys will serve a month in jail for using firearms on a public vehicle. They always get a month.

FELIX

What do you mean "always"?

DETECTIVE

This is the fifth time they've done this.

FELIX
The *fifth* time?

OSCAR
(*To Detective*)
That's a *five*-fecta.

Felix glares at him and Oscar steps away from him.

EXT. PARKING LOT

The two Detectives walking with Oscar and Felix.

DETECTIVE
There's an airport about five miles from here. You can't land in San Malina but there's one in Rockport. Then it's a twenty-minute cab drive to where you're going.

FELIX
See, Rockport is a name I would have remembered.

DETECTIVE
The flight should take you about forty minutes. I don't have a car to take you to the airport but we have a police transfer vehicle going by there.

FELIX
A police car? Finally a ride I'm going to feel safe in.

DETECTIVE
I hope you won't be offended by my saying I hope to God I never see either of you again. Now get outa here.

FELIX
(*Smiles*)
Thank you.

UNIFORMED POLICEMAN
If you both come with me, the vehicle's in the garage.

They start to walk with him.

FELIX
You know, Os—

OSCAR
If you say "I'm gonna miss them," I'll kill you in the vehicle.

THE DETECTIVE

He watches them go, then to second Detective.

DETECTIVE
Andy . . . if those guys commit a triple murder and rob a bank—just let 'em go.

SECOND DETECTIVE
Gotcha.

They walk off.

EXT. POLICE VAN

It pulls out of the garage.

INT. POLICE VAN

On one side, we see Oscar, Felix and the uniformed Policeman. On the other side, protected by a mesh wire fence, are two PRISONERS, chained, shackled, unshaven and as mean looking as they come.
   They stare angrily at Oscar and Felix. Oscar and Felix sort of smile back.

FELIX
(To prisoners)
Hi, there.

OSCAR
(Nods to them)
How you doin'?

FIRST CON
. . . Just great. How about you?

FELIX
Oh, a little tired. We had a rough trial.

SECOND CON
Aww, too bad. You got a cigarette?

FELIX
No. I . . . I don't smoke.

SECOND CON
Yeah. I should cut down too.
(To Oscar)
What about you?

OSCAR
No. I used to smoke cigars but I gave them up. . . . They were turning my teeth yellow.

SECOND CON
Yeah. I hate when that happens.

He gives a half smile revealing a mouth that is missing a few teeth in the front.

FIRST CON
So, you guys under arrest or what?

FELIX
No ... Well, yes. We were arrested three times this weekend but we were innocent.

FIRST AND SECOND CONS
Same here.

SECOND CON
So whattdya doin' in dis cage?

OSCAR
Well, this sheriff offered us a ride to the airport. We're kind of in a rush.

FELIX
We're flying to San Malina. Our kids are getting married.

FIRST CON
And this cop offers you a ride?

FELIX
Well, we had to give him our word that we would never *ever* return to this town again.

FIRST CON
(*Looks at the second*)
Why the fuck didn't *we* ask for that deal?

EXT. AIRPORT

The police van is pulling away as Oscar and Felix start in to the terminal.

OSCAR
If some travel agent booked this trip, we could sue them for a fortune.

FELIX
Everything happens for a reason, Oscar. We're not going through all this for nothing. I think there's some divine payoff at the end.

OSCAR
You want to buy my half? I'll sell it real cheap.

INT. TERMINAL

They walk to the gate. A dozen or so other people are waiting before they can board.

FELIX
Almost there, Oscar. We're actually going to make it. I can't believe it.

Then we hear a woman's voice behind them.

WOMAN
Oscar? Is that you?

They turn. They see the WOMAN. She's about fifty-five, very pretty, stylishly dressed, intelligent and easy to talk to.

WOMAN
(Smiles. A pretty smile)
It *is* you. I'm Felice Adams, Blanche's sister.

OSCAR
Felice? Oh, my God. I didn't recognize you. You haven't changed in thirty years. You look wonderful.

WOMAN
Oh. Thank you . . . I guess we're both going to the wedding, aren't we?

OSCAR
Yes. You live around here?

WOMAN
No. San Francisco. But you have to make four stops to get to Rockport.

Felix, with a big smile, is waiting to get introduced.

OSCAR
(Looks around)
Is your husband with you? What's his name again? Larry?

WOMAN
Barry . . . No. Barry passed away two years ago.

OSCAR
Oh, I'm very sorry. . . . You had two little daughters, didn't you?

WOMAN
And now two little granddaughters.

OSCAR
(Laughs)
Imagine that.
(Felix laughs too)
Oh. I'm sorry. This is my good friend, Felix Ungar. Felix, this is my ex-wife's
sister, Felice.

FELIX
How do you do.

FELICE
Felix Ungar? Oh, yes. I remember Blanche talking about you a lot.

FELIX
Yeah, well, I've changed since then.

FELICE
Haven't we all . . . Oh, they're boarding. See you on the plane.

She goes on ahead of them. They start to walk.

FELIX
(Aside)
Oscar, we have to talk.

OSCAR
About what?

FELIX
On the plane. *ON* the plane.

EXT. AIRFIELD

We see the small commuter plane take off and into the skies.

EXT./INT. THE PLANE

It carries about twenty-four passengers, capacity. It's not quite full. Felix at a window seat, third row, Oscar sitting next to him. Felice is sitting in the sixth row, the seat next to her is empty.
Felix turns back and smiles at her.

FELIX
Have a nice flight.

FELICE
(Looks up from her book)
Oh. Thank you. You too.
(She goes back into her book)

OSCAR
(To Felix)
All right, you want to talk, talk.

FELIX
Wait'll the seat belt sign goes off.

OSCAR
You can't talk with your seat belt on? Is that a new federal law?

FELIX
When it's still on, it could get bumpy and I don't want anything interrupting what I have to say.

THE SEATBELT SIGN

It goes from on to off.

FELIX AND OSCAR

They've both been watching it.

OSCAR
Okay. It's safe. We're bumpless. What is it you have to say?

FELIX
That's her. That's the woman.

OSCAR
What woman?

FELIX
The "somewhere, someplace in this world is the right woman for me"
woman. That's her.

OSCAR
Felice?

FELIX
Even the name is right. Felice—Felix. The first three letters are identical. We
match up. It's like an omen. I'm telling you, Oscar, she's the one.

OSCAR
Good. I'm very happy for the both of you.

FELIX
Don't mock this. I think we were meant to go through all that crap for me to
get on this plane and meet her today. I'm telling you, Oscar, this is the match
up I've been looking for.

OSCAR
(Nods)
Suppose she doesn't want to match up with you?
(He peeks back at her. She's still absorbed with her book. Then back to Felix)
. . . . Because right now her book is running about ten lengths ahead of you.

FELIX
Oscar, trust me. This one is written in the stars.

OSCAR
Yeah, well, until you get a fax, don't count on anything.

EXT. PLANE

We are flying over some beautiful West Coast scenery.

EXT./INT. PLANE

FELIX
(Peeks back, then to Oscar)
Okay. She put the book down. Now's my chance. . . . Think of a reason why I
should go over and sit down next to her.

OSCAR
I don't know. How about your seat is broken?

FELIX
I'm a bad liar. She'll know that I'm lying.

OSCAR
How about if I break your seat?

FELIX
No, no. I got it. Never mind.
(He gets up)
Wish me luck.

OSCAR
You're not going to tell me what your plan is?

FELIX
If I tell you and you don't like it, I'll lose confidence. Move your legs.

He gets by and into the aisle, then starts to walk back. As he passes her . . .

FELIX
Good day to fly, isn't it?

FELICE
(Smiles)
Yes. Perfect weather.

But he can't think or say the next word so he continues on and goes into the bathroom.

INT. BATHROOM

He's in and locks the door, then bangs his fist into the wall.

FELIX
What's wrong with me? Damn me to hell. I finally meet the right woman
and I can't say the right thing.
(He turns, looks into the mirror. A look of determination)

(At his reflection)
All right, you chicken-hearted gutless wimp. If you don't go back there and
sit next to her, you and I are through, you hear?

*He opens the door, steps out, straightens his tie, throws back his shoulders and takes
two steps and stops. He looks.*

FELICE'S SEAT

Oscar is sitting next to her. They seem to be deeply into conversation.
Felix walks back down the aisle, glares at Oscar and sits in his own seat.

EXT.—THE PLANE IS FLYING OVER MORE MOUNTAINOUS
AREAS

EXT./INT. PLANE

Oscar comes back and sits next to Felix again.

FELIX
Have a nice *chat,* old buddy pal dear close friend of mine?

OSCAR
Relax. I just set it all up. Go on back and sit down.

FELIX
What did you say to her?

OSCAR
I told her you were writing an article for the New York Sunday Times about
widowed women and womenless men. And you wondered if you could ask
her a few questions. She said absolutely. Go on, she's waiting for you.

FELIX
Why'd you tell her that?

OSCAR
Well, it was better than you going into the john and banging on the walls
again. . . . Are you going or do you want me to get the food trolley and *wheel*
you over?

FELIX
I'm going. I'm going.

He gets up, crosses down the aisle and stops at her seat.

. . . May I?

FELICE
(*Smiles*)
Please do.

He sits.

FELIX

First of all, I have to explain about that article I'm writing.

FELICE

What article?

FELIX

The one Oscar told you I was writing for the Sunday Times?

FELICE

He never told me that.

FELIX

(*Stunned*)

. . . Then what was he saying to you?

FELICE

That you wanted to meet me and couldn't think of a good reason to sit down next to me, and I said tell him to come over and sit. I'd like to meet him as well.

Felix looks dumbstruck. Then turns and looks at Oscar. Oscar is smiling, then winks at him.

COCKPIT OF PLANE

PILOT and COPILOT. Pilot on the speaker phone.

PILOT

Ladies and gentlemen, we should be arriving at Rockport's Barbra Streisand Airport in about twenty minutes. So just relax and enjoy the rest of our flight.

OSCAR

He is fast asleep in his seat.

FELIX AND FELICE

They are both laughing hard.

FELIX

. . . No, no. First the car caught fire and exploded and *then* we got the ride on the truck.

FELICE

. . . And that's when you got arrested for the second time?

FELIX

No. That was the first time. The second time was when Thelma and Holly's husbands, LeRoy and JayJay abducted all four of us from the bus.

They are enjoying this immensely.

EXT. A CAB ON THE ROAD

EXT./INT. CAB

The three of them in the back. Felice sitting in the middle.

FELIX

. . . No, I never use tarragon. Maybe a few bay leaves and just a hint of pesto sauce.

FELICE

Really? And how long do you let it simmer?

FELIX

Two, three minutes on a low flame. Ten seconds too much could be disastrous.

OSCAR

I don't mean to interrupt your Pasta Genovese but I think we're here.

EXT. THE WHITE HOUSE ON POINCIETTA STREET

Friends and guests have all arrived, gather on the lawn. Dozens of chairs are set in rows for the wedding service. The decorations, lanterns and floral arrangements are placed tastefully everywhere.

A small five-piece band is setting up. Maybe a pianist playing for the early arrivals.

Oscar, Felice and Felix get out of the cab. As Oscar pays, the cabbie puts Felice's bags out on the ground.

FELICE
(Looks at everything)
Oh, doesn't it look sweet?

FELIX
Is it too soon for me to get nervous or can I start now?
(To Oscar)
Is this exciting or what?

A YOUNG MAN takes Felice's bags and heads for the house. Oscar looks around, starts to sniff.

FELIX
(Sniffs too)
Yeah. Don't those flowers smell incredible?

OSCAR
I'm not smelling flowers. I smell trouble. I can smell it a mile away. Something's wrong here.

FELIX
Really? How come you never smelled it on the peach truck? Or on the bus? Or in the slowest Rolls Royce in the world? Relax, Oscar, let's get a drink.

OSCAR
Where's Blanche? Where's Frances? Where are the families? Why isn't someone here to meet us?

FELICE

I'm sure they're all tending to last-minute preparations. And things look like they're going very well. I'm dying for something to drink.

(She crosses to the outdoor bar)

THE HOUSE

FRED, Blanche's third husband comes out on the porch, sees Oscar and Felix, waves and comes walking quickly toward them.

FRED

Oscar? I'm Fred Wyman, Blanche's third husband.

OSCAR

(They shake hands)

Where's her *second* husband?

FRED

He's here with his third wife.

OSCAR

This is Felix Ungar. Hannah's father. Is everything all right?

FRED

All right? Oh, yes. Fine. Fine. . . . There's one problem that's come up but I'm sure it'll straighten out. Could you and Mr. Ungar come inside a minute?

As they follow Fred, Oscar gives a gloating look at Felix.

OSCAR

(To Felix as he points to his own nose)

This is the nose that knew the Braves would blow the '96 World Series.

FELIX

(Yells, waves to Felice, who is sipping champagne and talking to friends)

Felice! I'll be right back. Don't go 'way.

She smiles and shakes head "no."

INT. THE HOUSE

The boys follow Fred down a long hallway, through a den, through a dining room, through the kitchen, which is at a feverish pace with cooks, and then through another door to a small, enclosed patio, away from everyone else. There is BLANCHE, FRANCES and her new husband JACK.

The men are comforting the women. Blanche and Frances rise when they see the boys.

> **BLANCHE**
> Oh, Oscar. Thank God you're here.

> **FRANCES**
> Oh, Felix. What a mess.

She gives him a quick hug.

> **FELIX**
> Hello, Frances. You're looking wonderful. . . . What's going on?

> **FRANCES**
> Blanche, you tell him.

> **BLANCHE**
> Brucey is gone.

> **OSCAR**
> Gone? Gone where?

> **BLANCHE**
> He disappeared.

> **FRANCES**
> We can't find him.

> **BLANCHE**
> He wasn't in his room.

FRANCES

We looked everywhere.

BLANCHE

We even called the police.

The two women start to cry.

OSCAR

All right, don't cry. It's bad luck to cry before a wedding.

BLANCHE

No, it's only bad luck if the groom isn't here before the wedding.

FELIX

Did he leave a message? A note?

FRANCES

Nothing. Not a clue.

OSCAR

He'll show up. My kid never ducked out of anything.

FELIX

Where's Hannah? Is she all right? Can I see my daughter, please?

FRANCES

She's upstairs getting dressed. . . . We haven't told her.

FELIX

You haven't TOLD HER??? What were you waiting for? Her fifth
anniversary of being alone?

FRANCES

Don't yell at me.

FELIX

I wasn't yelling at you. I'm yelling at the situation.

FRANCES

God, you haven't changed in thirty years, have you?

FELIX

I don't believe this. I haven't seen the woman in half a century and she still hasn't finished the *last* fight we had.

OSCAR

All right, can everyone stop acting like children here?

BLANCHE

Children? You think we're children? We've been preparing this wedding for three months and you take a casual joy ride to get here? Patronizing women again, Oscar?

OSCAR

Don't yell at me, Blanche. You got two other husbands here to do that. . . . Felix, can we go in the other room a minute? I need to talk to you.

He leads Felix out into another room and closes the door.

FELIX

How about that Frances? I'd love to divorce her again, I swear. . . . So what do you think has happened?

OSCAR

My honest opinion?

FELIX

Yes.

OSCAR

I don't know.

FELIX

So what are you calling me out here for?

OSCAR

I thought maybe *you'd* have an idea.

FELIX

If *I* had an idea, I would have called *you* out here. . . . So what do we do?

OSCAR

We'll have to wait and see. The worst that can happen is we'll have to postpone the wedding.

FELIX

Postpone?? You think I'm going to let my daughter be humiliated in front of the whole world because of your ditzy son?

OSCAR

Hey! Watch what you say about my son. Maybe it's your Hannah that's the wacky one.

FELIX

Hannah wacky?? My Hannah wacky??

OSCAR

Stop repeating it. Sounds like an Hawaiian hotel. . . . One of them caused this, I don't know which one.

FELIX

And I'm saying, if he breaks her heart, that boy will have to deal with me.

OSCAR

Are you threatening to get physical with my kid?

FELIX

If that's what it takes.

They are now nose to nose.

OSCAR

Get your nose off my nose before I sneeze your brains into a tiny Kleenex.

FELIX

That's it! That's it, Oscar. . . .

The door opens. We hear a helicopter overhead. Frances and Blanche come in.

BLANCHE
They found him.

FELIX
They found him? Oscar, they found him.

FRANCES
A police helicopter just spotted him.

OSCAR
Where is he, for God's sake?

EXT. THE HELICOPTER

We see it flying over the house, making low passes.

POV. THE HELICOPTER

Looking down, we see the grounds, the guests and now Felix, Oscar, Frances and Blanche and others all looking up. The copter makes a turn and then swoops down toward the roof. Bruce is sitting on the roof wearing jeans, sneakers and a T-shirt. He is sitting tightly against the chimney, out of sight of everyone below. He waves off the copter and turns his face away.

BULLHORN FROM HELICOPTER

BULLHORN
He's on the roof!

INT. THE HOUSE

Oscar, Felix and the others all rush up the stairs. On the landing.

OSCAR
Which is his room?

BLANCHE
(Points)
That one there.

They all follow Oscar to the door. He stops.

OSCAR
(To others)
This is not a coffee klatsch. He's my son, I'll talk to him alone.

BLANCHE
He's my son too. He'll listen to me.

OSCAR
Is that why he's up on the roof?

He opens the door slowly and goes in.

INT. THE GUEST ROOM

Oscar crosses to the open window and leans out.

THE ROOF

Bruce is still sitting near the chimney.

OSCAR
(Looking out)
Beautiful day, isn't it?

BRUCE
Yeah.

OSCAR
I hope you don't think I'm meddling but . . . were you planning on coming to
the wedding today?

BRUCE

I'm thinking about it.

Oscar sits on the sill.

OSCAR

Nervous, heh? Listen, everyone gets nervous before they get married. The night before my wedding, I tried to join the Peace Corps in Kenya.

BRUCE

. . . I think I'd be making a big mistake.

OSCAR

Why is that?

BRUCE

Because I don't trust marriage. Look at everyone here. My own family. Mom's been married three times. You were married once and then never again for thirty years. Hers were too many and yours not enough. What's wrong with it that frightens everyone so much?

OSCAR

Well, it's like baseball. Either you can play or you can't. I couldn't play and your mother *could* play but she kept getting traded all the time.

BRUCE

That's not the answer I'm looking for.

OSCAR

Then why'd you wait so long to ask the question?

BRUCE

Because it's what I thought I wanted. Until I saw all the divorcees gather here. And now I know it's not what I want.

OSCAR

You sure?

BRUCE
Yes. I'm sure.

OSCAR
Then get out of it. Don't do it, Brucey.

Bruce looks at him.

BRUCE
Do you mean it?

OSCAR
Absolutely. Because you'll live your life out regretting this day forever. Get out, Bruce. She's young, she's pretty, she'll find someone else. But you're my son. Don't do this terrible thing to yourself. . . . Let me go talk to the others, I'll figure out what to say.

He comes in and crosses to the door. Bruce climbs into the room.

BRUCE
The only thing is, I really love her.

OSCAR
Sure you love her. *Now!* So you'll have two years of excitement and forty-five years of hell. Trust me, Brucey.

He turns to open the door.

BRUCE
I'll *always* love her. She's the best thing that's ever happened to me.

OSCAR
Would you be willing to gamble your life on that? I know I haven't been there enough for you, Bruce, but this is the best advice I'll ever give you. Not getting married today is the right thing for you to do.

BRUCE

Maybe right for you, Dad, but it's wrong for me. . . . Tell everyone I'm
getting dressed.

OSCAR
(Relieved)

Thank God you said that. I didn't know how long I could keep up talking
like an asshole.

They cross to each other, embrace.

INT. BEDROOM

*HANNAH, the bride to be, is being attended to by the DRESSMAKER's last-
minute retouches. Hannah looks ravishing. A knock on the door.*

MARIA
(Latina)

Whoever it is, go 'way. We not ready.

FELIX
(Voice through door)

Not even for your old man?

HANNAH

Dad? Oh, God! . . . Maria, let him in. Hurry.

*Maria crosses to door, mumbling to herself in Spanish. She opens it. Felix comes in
and looks at Hannah. He stops, overwhelmed.*

MARIA

I come back soon. If you smudge her dress, I kill you.

She goes, closes the door.

FELIX
(Misty-eyed)
Oh, dear God. I have just seen Heaven and it's in living color.

HANNAH
(Beaming)
Do you like it?

FELIX
I would say "yes" if I could just get the lump out of my throat first. Can I hug you?

HANNAH
You better. Because if you didn't make it, I would have postponed.

They embrace.

HANNAH
Have you seen Bruce? Isn't he terrific?

FELIX
Er, yes. I didn't get a chance to talk to him. He was—busy.

HANNAH
On the roof? I know.

FELIX
You knew?

HANNAH
I sent him there. He started getting the jitters and I said, "Hey, Bruce. Don't bother me. Go sleep on the roof. I've got more important things to do."

FELIX
(Smiles)
No kidding? Good for you.

HANNAH
So was it a terrible trip?

FELIX

Well, if you asked me that question four hours ago I would have said, the pits. But something happened on the plane and suddenly everything's coming up roses.

HANNAH

You met someone?

FELIX

I'll save it for later. I don't want to keep you. . . . As a matter of fact, I *can't* keep you anymore, can I?

HANNAH

Well, you could stay closer if you moved to California.

FELIX

That's funny. Because I was just thinking about checking out San Francisco.

A knock on the door.

I'll get it.
(He starts for door)
Oh, I hope you don't mind my giving the bride away dressed like this.

HANNAH

You look great to me.

He opens the door. Maria comes in.

MARIA

Mr. Ungar? This suitcase jus' come for you.

Felix, amazed and delighted, takes his suitcase.

FELIX

On second thought, maybe I'll spiff it up a bit.

He goes.

EXT. THE FRONT LAWN

The wedding is in progress. Felix is wearing his black afternoon formal. Oscar stands behind the now dressed Bruce, with Blanche at his side. Frances stands beside Felix.

JUSTICE OF PEACE
. . . Then with the power vested in me by the state of California, I now pronounce you man and wife. You may kiss the bride.

Bruce gives Hannah a loving kiss as the guests applaud and whistle. The fathers give their kids each a kiss. Then Felix gives Frances a kiss on the cheek. Then sneezes.

FRANCES
Still allergic to my perfume?

FELIX
No, that's gone. It just triggered an old memory in my sinuses.

He turns and looks for Felice. She sees him and waves. He crosses to her.
  Oscar kisses Blanche.

OSCAR
Congratulations, Blanche.

BLANCHE
I'm sorry I yelled at you, Oscar.

OSCAR
Nah. I deserved it. I forgot why but it's not important.
(The music starts)
Come on. Dance with me. I'll show you what you missed.

THE PARTY

Felix dances with Felice. Oscar dances with Blanche. Hannah dances with Bruce. Others get up to dance.

IT'S DUSK

The party's been going for a while. Felix is dancing with Hannah.

HANNAH
Dad, the silver tray is gorgeous.

FELIX
So are you.

HANNAH
And Bruce told me what you gave him. That is so generous.

FELIX
I wish it was ten times that much. Because I've got the most beautiful woman
at the party.
(He looks around)

HANNAH
What are you looking for?

FELIX
The second most beautiful.
(He sees Felice dancing with an attractive man)
Oh, oh. Competition.

HANNAH
I know her.

FELIX
She's your mother-in-law's sister. Now your aunt-in-law. . . . Could also be
your new stepmother.

HANNAH
Good. Keep it in the family.

Bruce taps Felix on the shoulder.

BRUCE
(To Felix)
Felice wants you to rescue her.

FELIX
She said that?

Felice nods to him. Felix gives Hannah to Bruce, then crosses and taps Felice's PARTNER on the shoulder.

FELIX
May I?

PARTNER
You again? You've tapped me out six times.

FELIX
Sorry. You know how husbands are about their wives.

PARTNER
That's news to me. I'm her cousin.

Felice laughs and she dances off with Felix.

LATER THAT NIGHT

The party is almost over. The band is playing some mellow oldie as a few couples remain, some still dancing. Blanche, Frances and their husbands at a table having a final champagne.
  Hannah talking to her bridesmaids.
  Oscar and Bruce sitting on the steps of the porch.

BRUCE
(Looking at Hannah)
Isn't she incredible, Pop.

Oscar nods, then takes out an envelope.

OSCAR

Bruce, I have something here for you and Hannah.

BRUCE

Pop, before you do that, I know you're strapped for cash. Just the gesture is enough for Hannah and me.

OSCAR

Who's strapped? I don't spend any money. The ladies in my poker game fill up my freezer every week. I have chicken soup ice cubes. . . . What I have here is not cash. . . . Please take it.

Bruce takes it and opens it. He takes out three baseball cards, looking a little worn.

BRUCE

Baseball cards? Great. You know I always saved them.

OSCAR

Not these. I've had these since before you were born. First editions, signed by Joe DiMaggio. Mickey Mantle, rookie year and Babe Ruth in his last year. . . . Today they're worth about twenty-two thousand.

BRUCE

No way, Pop. I can't take them.

OSCAR

Then hold them for me. Until your kids are eighteen. It'll buy them a few weeks in college.

BRUCE
(Moved)
. . . You're the greatest, Pop.

OSCAR

I know, but it only comes out once in a while. . . . I'm tired. Walk me in.

They get up, walk toward the house.

BRUCE

No chance of your moving out here?

OSCAR

To where? Santa Yocinta Malinta Calienta Malaguena? I'm not gonna learn
a new language just to find my way home at night....

They keep walking.

EXT.—LONG SHOT OF THE PARTY

*The only ones left dancing to the music of the remaining pianist are Bruce and
Hannah.*

INT. BEDROOM—NIGHT

*A big double bed. Oscar is already in bed. Felix, in the bathroom, is singing "Every-
thing's coming up roses." ... The light goes out and he comes out wearing fresh pajamas.*

FELIX

Oooh, it feels good to have clean pajamas on again.... I am going to sleep
my little toesies off tonight.

Felix gets into bed, wriggles around, annoying Oscar.

FELIX

God, what a wedding. And I'm so glad the kids loved the silver tray.... You
never told me what you gave them, Os. Not that it's any of my business.

OSCAR

I gave them baseball cards.

FELIX

Really? You think they're going to have time to play cards on their
honeymoon?

OSCAR

Felix, tomorrow night I'm going to be sleeping in my own bed. It's not a great bed but I love it. Because it never talks during the night.

FELIX

I'm sorry. It's just that, well . . . it might be another seventeen years before we see each other again.

OSCAR

Good. We'll make it a date.
Look, the bus leaves for the L.A. airport at nine in the morning. I want to get some sleep.

FELIX

Oh. Didn't I tell you? No bus. Leece is hiring a limo to get us all to the airport.

OSCAR

Leece? Who's Leece?

FELIX

Felice. But I started calling her Leece and she liked it.

OSCAR

Really? What does she call you? *Lix?*

FELIX

Oh. Something else. I'm not going back to New York yet. I'm going to stay up in San Fran for a while.

OSCAR

San Fran?? . . . Lix and Leece in San Fran? . . . What's going on?

FELIX

Who knows? May stay a few days, may stay forever . . . We really hit it off tonight, Oscar.

OSCAR

I've heard you say that before.

FELIX

Well, this may be the *last* time you ever hear me say it.

OSCAR

Good. I hope so. I really do. Well, I'm exhausted. . . . G.N.

FELIX

G.N.?

OSCAR

Good night.

EXT. THE L.A. AIRPORT

INT. L.A.X. TERMINAL

Oscar, Felix and Felice enter the terminal. Oscar looks at his ticket.

OSCAR

I'm at Gate 46. Where's that?

FELICE

That's down at that end. We're at the other end.

Oscar nods. There is a moment of awkwardness, of how to say good-bye.

FELICE

Felix, I'll change your ticket. Give you and Oscar a chance to say good-bye.

FELIX

What? . . . Oh. Yeah. Thanks.

FELICE

Good-bye, Oscar. Have a wonderful flight.

OSCAR

And the same to you, Leece.

She smiles and walks away to the counter. Oscar and Felix alone, still wondering what to say.

OSCAR

. . . So where you gonna live? With her?

FELIX

No. Of course not. . . . She has a little guest house in the back.

OSCAR

She looks like she has a lot of dogs. You're going to be walking a lot of dogs, Felix.

FELIX

You think I'm making a mistake?

OSCAR

I don't give that advice twice on the same weekend.

FELIX

It could be my last chance, Os. I just want to give it a try.
(Oscar nods)
Hey, if it doesn't work, I'll just go back to my old life . . . whatever that was.

OSCAR

I wish you the best, Felix.

FELIX

You do?

OSCAR

Of course my best doesn't always mean much.

FELIX

It does to me.

He puts his arms around Oscar, embraces, his cheek to Oscar's cheek. He holds on.

OSCAR

Okay, that's enough. . . . Felix, stop. She'll think you and I had something going.

Felix pulls away, then turns and goes quickly.

HIGH UP

We see Oscar walking in his direction and Felix and Felice in the opposite direction. Felix turns and gives Oscar one last look, then continues on.

EXT. A FULL MOON

It is bright, shining down on Sarasota, Florida. We see the palm trees on the way down, then the exterior of Oscar's condo, at night. We move in toward the window. The poker game is in progress.
    The usual guests. Abe, Hattie, Esther, Millie, Wanda and Flossie.
    Oscar is putting some food down on the poker table.

OSCAR

Who gets the bagel with the tofu cream cheese?

MILLIE

That's mine.

OSCAR

And the soy bean facsimile corned beef sandwich?

ABE

That's me. . . . This doesn't have salt, does it?

OSCAR

Just a tinge. But the box said it expired two years ago, it's safe.

FLOSSIE

Are you in this game, Oscar?

OSCAR
Yes. I'm in for twenty cents.

FLOSSIE
You didn't look at your cards.

OSCAR
At these prices, I'll take the plunge.

WANDA
(Struggles with fork and cake)
This cheesecake is hard as a rock.

OSCAR
That's the wax model they keep in the window. If you like the way it looks,
I'll order it.

ESTHER
So tell us about the wedding. What did they serve?

OSCAR
(Sits, looks at cards)
Veal Alphonso.

ESTHER
How do they make it?

OSCAR
A guy named Alphonso comes in early.

The doorbell rings. Oscar gets up.

I'll get it. I ordered pizza.

HATTIE
For tonight?

OSCAR
No. From before the wedding. I forgot to cancel it.

He opens it. A forlorn-looking Felix stands there.

FELIX
Hi, Os . . . I was in the neighborhood so I thought I'd drop in.

OSCAR
What a surprise.
(Looks over his shoulder)
Is Felice with you?

FELIX
No. It didn't work out. The woman left her clothes all over the floor, always ran out of towels, bobby pins in the bed. I just couldn't hack it. . . . Am I disturbing you?

OSCAR
No. No. Come on in.

Felix goes back into hall, gets two heavy suitcases and brings them in the apartment. Oscar looks at suitcases suspiciously.

FELIX
(To ladies)
Hi.

OSCAR
Girls, I'd like you to meet the father of the bride, Felix Ungar. Felix, these are my poker buddies.

FELIX
Gee, I hope I'm not interrupting the game.

The women smile, a little flirtatiously.

HATTIE
No. My goodness, not at all.

WANDA
It's a distinct pleasure to meet you.

ESTHER
(Squints)
I can't see him. Is he cute?

OSCAR
Girls, can you excuse us for one minute? Felix, can we have a word inside?

As they leave, the women buzz like bees with their heads over the table. All except Abe.

THE BEDROOM

OSCAR
What's with the suitcases?

FELIX
I gave up my apartment in New York.

OSCAR
To live in Sarasota?

FELIX
They have hospitals here too, you know.

OSCAR
Are you planning to move in with me again, Felix? Because it didn't work the last time.

FELIX
No, no. Just till I get my own place. . . . Although we could save a lot of money splitting expenses.

OSCAR
Nothing's changed, Felix. I'm still a pig and you're still a human vacuum cleaner.

FELIX
I know . . . Look, if you don't think it would work, just say "No."

OSCAR
No!

Felix looks at him, nods.

FELIX
Okay . . . So I'll go.
(He starts to go)

OSCAR
(Watches him)
. . . I didn't say "Go." I said "No." . . . All right, we'll try it for a few weeks.
But the minute you try matching up my socks, we call it quits.

FELIX
(Smiles)
It's a deal. . . . Go on. Go back to your game. I'll get my bags and hang up a
few things.

Oscar leaves.

MILLIE
He looks so sweet.

HATTIE
If he's looking, I've got a spare bedroom I don't use.

OSCAR
Ladies, it's possible that in five weeks you'll *all* move out of Sarasota,
Florida. . . . Whose bet is it?

Felix comes out, his jacket is off.

FELIX

Don't mind me, folks. Just going to get a beer.

(He looks down)

Oh. Is this your napkin?

(He picks it up, gives it to Esther)

. . . That sandwich looks a little limp. I could retoast it for you in a second.

ABE

Really? I wouldn't mind.

FELIX

No trouble at all.

He picks up the plate and goes off into the kitchen.

OSCAR

This is the *biggest Goddamndest* deja vu anyone ever had. . . . Can we play cards, please?

The game resumes as the camera pulls back, slowly out of the room, out of the house, into Sarasota, still on the game. . . .

FADE-OUT

THE END